WORLD
HISTORY SERIES

Viking
Conquests

Titles in the World History Series

The Abolition of American Slavery
The Age of Augustus
The Age of Exploration
The Age of Feudalism
The Age of Napoléon
The Age of Pericles
The Alamo
America in the 1960s
The American Revolution
Ancient America
Ancient Chinese Dynasties
Ancient Greece
The Ancient Near East
The Assyrian Empire
The Battle of the
    Little Bighorn
The Black Death
The Byzantine Empire
Caesar's Conquest of Gaul
The California Gold Rush
The Chinese Cultural
    Revolution
The Civil Rights Movement
The Cold War
The Collapse of the
    Roman Republic
Colonial America
The Computer Revolution
The Conquest of Mexico
The Constitution and the
    Founding of America
The Crimean War
The Cuban Missile Crisis
The Early Middle Ages
Egypt of the Pharaohs
The Enlightenment
The Great Depression
Greek and Roman Mythology
Greek and Roman Science

Greek and Roman Sport
Greek and Roman Theater
The History of Medicine
The History of Rock & Roll
The History of Slavery
The Incan Empire
The Internment of the Japanese
The Italian Renaissance
The Late Middle Ages
The Making of the Atom Bomb
The Mayan Civilization
The Mexican-American War
The Mexican Revolution
The Mexican War of
    Independence
The Mongol Empire
The Persian Empire
Prohibition
The Punic Wars
The Reagan Years
The Reformation
The Renaissance
The Rise and Fall of the
    Soviet Union
The Roaring Twenties
Roosevelt and the
    New Deal
Russia of the Tsars
The Salem Witch Trials
The Space Race
The Spanish-American War
The Stone Age
The Titanic
Traditional Africa
Twentieth-Century Science
Viking Conquests
The War of 1812
World War II in the Pacific

WORLD HISTORY SERIES ■ ■ ■

Viking Conquests

by
David Schaffer

LUCENT BOOKS
SAN DIEGO, CALIFORNIA

THOMSON
✴ ™
GALE

Detroit • New York • San Diego • San Francisco
Boston • New Haven, Conn. • Waterville, Maine
London • Munich

For Nancy and Helena,
who fill my life with joy.

Library of Congress Cataloging-in-Publication Data

Schaffer, David.
    Viking Conquests / by David Schaffer.
        p. cm.—(World history series)
    Summary: A historical overview of the Vikings, whose
force and military strength combined with a strong interest in
trade and commercial activity that brought them success
through much of Europe during the Middle Ages.
    ISBN 1-59018-322-X (hardback. : alk. paper)
    1. Viking—Juvenile literature. 2. Middle Ages—Juvenile
literature—History—Juvenile literature. [1. Vikings. 2. Middle
Ages—History.] I. Title. II. Series.
DL65.S34 2002
940.1—dc21

2001004232

Copyright 2002 by Lucent Books
an imprint of The Gale Group
10911 Technology Place, San Diego, CA 92127

Printed in the U.S.A.

Contents

Foreword

Each year on the first day of school, nearly every history teacher faces the task of explaining why his or her students should study history. One logical answer to this question is that exploring what happened in our past explains how the things we often take for granted—our customs, ideas, and institutions—came to be. As statesman and historian Winston Churchill put it, "Every nation or group of nations has its own tale to tell. Knowledge of the trials and struggles is necessary to all who would comprehend the problems, perils, challenges, and opportunities which confront us today." Thus, a study of history puts modern ideas and institutions in perspective. For example, though the founders of the United States were talented and creative thinkers, they clearly did not invent the concept of democracy. Instead, they adapted some democratic ideas that had originated in ancient Greece and with which the Romans, the British, and others had experimented. An exploration of these cultures, then, reveals their very real connection to us through institutions that continue to shape our daily lives.

Another reason often given for studying history is the idea that lessons exist in the past from which contemporary societies can benefit and learn. This idea, although controversial, has always been an intriguing one for historians. Those who agree that society can benefit from the past often quote philosopher George Santayana's famous statement, "Those who cannot remember the past are condemned to repeat it." Historians who subscribe to Santayana's philosophy believe that, for example, studying the events that led up to the major world wars or other significant historical events would allow society to chart a different and more favorable course in the future.

Just as difficult as convincing students of the importance of studying history is the search for useful and interesting supplementary materials that present historical events in a context that can be easily understood. The volumes in Lucent Books' World History series attempt to present a broad, balanced, and penetrating view of the march of history. Ancient Egypt's important wars and rulers, for example, are presented against the rich and colorful backdrop of Egyptian religious, social, and cultural developments. The series engages the reader by enhancing historical events with these cultural contexts. For example, in *Ancient Greece*, the text covers the role of women in that society. Slavery is discussed in *The Roman Empire*, as well as how slaves earned their freedom. The numerous and varied aspects of everyday life in these and other societies are explored in each volume of the series. Additionally, the series covers the major political, cultural, and philosophical ideas as the torch of civilization is passed from ancient Mesopotamia and Egypt, through Greece, Rome, Medieval Europe, and other world cultures to the modern day.

The material in the series is formatted in a thorough, precise, and organized manner. Each volume offers the reader a comprehensive and clearly written overview of an important historical event or period. The topic under discussion is placed in a broad, historical context. For example, *The Italian Renaissance* begins with a discussion of the High Middle Ages and the loss of central control that allowed certain Italian cities to develop artistically. The book ends by looking forward to the Reformation and interpreting the societal changes that grew out of the Renaissance. Thus, students are not only involved in an historical era, but also enveloped by the events leading up to that era and the events following it.

One important and unique feature in the World History series is the primary and secondary source quotations that richly supplement each volume. These quotes are useful in a number of ways. First, they allow students access to sources they would not normally be exposed to because of the difficulty and obscurity of the original source. The quotations range from interesting anecdotes to farsighted cultural perspectives and are drawn from historical witnesses both past and present. Second, the quotes demonstrate how and where historians themselves derive their information on the past as they strive to reach a consensus on historical events. Lastly, all of the quotes are footnoted, familiarizing students with the citation process and allowing them to verify quotes and/or look up the original source if the quote piques their interest.

Finally, the books in the World History series provide a detailed launching point for further research. Each book contains a bibliography specifically geared toward student research. A second, annotated bibliography introduces students to all the sources the author consulted when compiling the book. A chronology of important dates gives students an overview, at a glance, of the topic covered. Where applicable, a glossary of terms is included.

In short, the series is designed not only to acquaint readers with the basics of history, but also to make them aware that their lives are part of an ongoing human saga. Perhaps then they will come to the same realization as famed historian Arnold Toynbee. In his monumental work, *A Study of History*, he wrote about becoming aware of history flowing through him in a mighty current, and of his own life "welling like a wave in the flow of this vast tide."

IMPORTANT DATES IN THE HISTORY OF THE VIKING CONQUESTS

ca. 835
Viking raid on the English island of Sheppey. First of many consecutive years when at least one Viking raid was reported in the *Anglo-Saxon Chronicle*.

793
Viking raid on Lindisfarne monastery, Holy Island, England.

845
First Viking attack on Paris, resulting in earliest known danegeld payment to Vikings.

850
First Vikings settle on English soil between raiding seasons.

852
Earliest recorded Viking raid in Russian territory at Novgorod. Norwegians recapture Dublin and begin new surge of power in Ireland.

865
The Great Viking Army arrives in England and begins their conquest of the northern and eastern regions of the country.

871
Agreement between English king Alfred and the Vikings regarding the division of England between the Danes and the English that results in the formation of the Danelaw, an officially recognized area in England under Viking control.

700   750   800   850   900

794–799
First recorded Viking raids in Ireland and western continental Europe.

819
The Vikings first establish a base on the island of Noirmoutier at the mouth of the Loire River in western continental Europe.

841
Establishment of Dublin, the first Viking longphort in Ireland.

ca. 830–835
Viking chieftain Turgeis leads intensified inland raids in Ireland.

856–857
The "Great Invasion" of Frankia, including the second major attack on Paris.

ca. 855–860
Viking raids become heavy around the Dnieper River. The Vikings come to power in Kiev.

860
First attack against Constantinople by Vikings based around Kiev.

862
Rurik and the Rus take control of northern Russia with their power center at Novgorod.

885
After a resumption of heavy raiding in western continental Europe for several years, the Vikings launch their third major attack on Paris.

ca. 880
Oleg takes over Kiev and unites it with Novgorod, becomes first Russian crown ruler.

878
English Vikings, led by Guthrum, invade and almost conquer Wessex.

891
The Battle of Louvain marks an end to significant Viking activity in Frankia in the ninth century. The Vikings in Brittany are driven out by Breton forces united under Alain of Vannes.

902
Dublin Vikings driven out of Ireland.

933
Third and final territorial concessions by the Franks to the Normans.

970
Second Viking attack against Constantinople. First trade agreement between Rus Vikings and Byzantines.

954
Erik Bloodaxe, last Viking king of York, is deposed.

1014
Danish king Swein Forkbeard conquers England; large contingent of Vikings assembled in Ireland is defeated by Irish forces loyal to Brian Boru in the Battle of Clontarf.

999
Irish Vikings defeated in the Battle of Glenn Máma; Brian Boru occupies Dublin.

991
English king Ethelred makes the first major danegeld payment to come from the throne of England: ten thousand pounds of silver. Danegeld payments grow to even bigger sizes through 1013.

988
Grand Prince of Kiev Vladimir adapts Orthodox Christianity as the official religion of Russia. Varangian Guard is formed by agreement between Vladimir and the Byzantine emperor.

900 **950** **1000** **1050** **1100**

911
Official formation of Normandy occurs with the Treaty of St. Clair-sur-Epte.

915–920
Vikings resume raiding in Ireland. New Dublin settlement established by Norwegian Vikings, who later capture the city of York from the Danish.

924
Second territorial concessions by the Franks to the Normans.

941–944
Renewed heavy Viking raiding in Byzantium. Third and fourth attacks upon Constantinople. Rus and Byzantines reconcile, renew trade and access agreements.

980
Irish Vikings defeated in the Battle of Tara. Heavy Viking raiding activity resumes in England.

1016
Swein Forkbeard's son Canute is recognized as the king of all of England; he brings peace and stability to the country during his reign. He later reigns over the largest Viking empire in history.

1066
Harold Godwinsson is crowned king of England. Forces led by Norwegian king Harald Hardrada invade England and are defeated by Godwinsson at the Battle of Stamford Bridge. Norman forces led by Duke William follow immediately with another invasion and defeat Godwinsson's English forces at the Battle of Hastings, signifying the closing of the Viking era.

Terror from a Pagan Race

June 8, 793, probably started much the same as every other day for the Christian monks at the Lindisfarne monastery on Holy Island, England. Like monks throughout Europe during the medieval period, those at Lindisfarne led lives that were remarkably quiet and mostly unexciting. They spent almost all their time in seclusion at their monastery. Among the few people in Europe who were able to read and write, they studied the Bible and wrote about historical events. Devoutly religious, they also spent considerable time in prayer and meditation. Some monks farmed to provide food for their monasteries.

The times, however, were not peaceful in Europe. The fall of the Roman Empire in the fifth century resulted in much of Europe declining into instability and widespread conflict for hundreds of years. The Roman Empire had included a large portion of Europe. The Romans' dominating military strength and the economic benefits that came with belonging to their empire tended to produce relative

Historians consider the Viking attack on the Lindisfarne monastery (pictured) to mark the beginning of the Viking age.

peace and prosperity within the large area they controlled. During the rule of the Romans, much of Europe enjoyed a level of civilization and affluence that it had previously never known. People were fairly comfortable, and there was little threat of being attacked or ravaged by warring armies or factions. After the Romans converted to Christianity in the fourth century, clergymen—like monks—throughout the empire gained status as people especially important and worthy of protection.

After the Romans lost power in Europe, the continent entered into a period when local and factional military conflicts became commonplace. With no powerful ruling authority like the Romans to restrain them, rival kingdoms and armies loyal to different lords and vassals battled with each other. Enemies routinely raided and invaded each other's territories. However, Christian monks continued to be mostly protected from these conflicts. The Christian religion that the Romans had brought to the areas within their empire remained powerful even after their rule ended, and even the fiercest warriors usually respected those who dedicated their lives to that religion. To be sure the sacred monasteries were safe, large walls and other protections were built around them. Many were located along seacoasts. At this time large, powerful navies did not exist among the major kingdoms of Europe, so it was believed that the oceans would provide additional protection from attack.

It therefore must have come as quite a shock to the monks at Lindisfarne when, on that June day, seemingly out of nowhere, a massive number of ships with ferocious-looking dragon heads suddenly appeared along the shores, carrying vicious rampaging warriors. Unlike other warriors who may have attacked nearby but left the monastery alone, these newcomers ravaged Lindisfarne, slashed and killed many of the people living there, and made off with as much money and other valuable items as they could. They then returned to their boats and disappeared over the horizon just as quickly as they came.

Historians generally consider the attack on Lindisfarne to be the beginning of the Viking age. Word of the horror that the Norse raiders inflicted, and the swiftness and ease with which they could attack from open oceans, stirred awe and fear among those who lived in these areas. An eighth-century scholar named Alcuin wrote the following description of the Lindisfarne attack in a letter to the king of the Northumbria region of England:

> Lo, it is some 350 years that we and our forefathers have inhabited this most lovely land, and never before has such terror appeared in Britain as we have now suffered from a pagan race, nor was it thought that such an inroad from the sea could be made.[1]

Descriptions such as this led to the image of the Vikings or Norsemen as a ruthless, savage people, completely uncivilized and thoroughly warlike in nature. This image persisted for several centuries thereafter.

Over time, however, a different and more complete picture of the Vikings has

Early descriptions of the Vikings depicted them as ruthless, savage, uncivilized, and warlike in nature. This image persisted for several centuries after the Viking age.

emerged. From new archaeological evidence and the widespread study of *The Icelandic Sagas* (histories of the Vikings written in the twelfth through fourteenth centuries), the Vikings have been revealed as expert tradesmen, fishermen, and craftsmen. They have also come to be credited as early pioneers in the creation and development of the legal trial and court procedures used in much of the modern world, and as among the earliest cultures to embrace representative legislative government. Historians now recognize the Norse as a multitalented, socially progressive civilization that left a lasting, if often violent, impact on the entire world.

Chapter

1 The Birth and Formation of Viking Culture

The Anglo-Saxon Chronicle, a historical document that recounts events in England during the medieval period, is a major source of information for Viking activity on the island of Great Britain. This passage is taken from the entry for the year 793, the year of the Lindisfarne raid:

> In this year terrible portents [omens] appeared in Northumbria and miserably frightened the inhabitants: these were exceptional flashes of lightning, and fiery dragons were seen flying in the air, and soon followed a great famine, and after that in the same year the harrying of the heathen miserably destroyed God's church in Lindisfarne by rapine [plunder] and slaughter.[2]

It was not the first time such an attack had been made by the Norsemen, the people who would come to be known as the Vikings. The *Chronicle* records another Norse raid in England four years earlier. Raids by the Norse on tribes living along the southern part of the Baltic Sea and on islands in the North Sea may have begun as early as the seventh century. However, after the raid on Lindisfarne, these kinds of attacks, for which the Vikings became

legendary, grew steadily in number. They occurred in many places throughout England, Ireland, and continental Europe. In some places, Vikings who came to raid stayed and settled, sometimes gaining control of the areas they occupied. Other times, they simply looted and moved on. Regardless of whether they stayed or merely pillaged, the Vikings had a significant and lasting impact on Western civilization and world history.

UNDERSTANDING THE VIKINGS

To understand the Vikings and how they became so important, it is necessary to know something about how their society originated and developed. For many centuries before the Viking era, the Norse lived in their homelands, and many of them prospered. They traveled throughout the known Western world and were knowledgeable of its people and their customs, but for thousands of years the Vikings showed no great interest in raiding or conquering outside their local areas. A combination of conditions in their homelands, their traditional beliefs and values, and the lack of strong governmental and

THE BIRTH AND FORMATION OF VIKING CULTURE ■ 13

SNORRI STURLUSON

There is precious little written information from Norse sources about the Viking era and the years leading up to it. *The Icelandic Sagas,* while largely fantastical, do represent most of the written historical accounts of that period from the Norse point of view. Most sagas are anonymous, but history does record the author of *Heimskringla: History of the Kings of Norway.* That author is Snorri Sturluson, an Icelander who lived in the late twelfth and early thirteenth centuries and was of great importance in his country's early history.

Around the age of four, Sturluson was adopted by Iceland's most prestigious citizen, Jón Loptsson, and taken to live at his estate, Oddi. At that time Oddi was a great center of culture and learning in Iceland. Sturluson also traveled to Norway and Sweden and met with royal Scandinavian leaders. Perhaps the most learned Icelander of his time, Sturluson also wrote other works during the early twelfth century when he was composing *Heimskringla.* These included the *Prose Edda,* a book about an ancient Norse form of poetry called skaldic verse, which included some samples of Sturluson's own skalds.

Among his countrymen, Sturluson was so revered that he was chosen to head the governing body known as the *Althing.* This was a group of Icelanders who met every year to make laws and decisions affecting Iceland's population. Iceland's Althing is credited as being a forerunner of modern-day parliaments and other representative government bodies like the U.S. Congress.

military leadership throughout much of Europe during the medieval period prompted the Norse to launch the ventures that produced the Viking era.

The Norse people lived and developed their society in Scandinavia, the area in northern Europe and the North Atlantic Ocean that includes the present-day nations of Norway, Sweden, Denmark, Finland, and Iceland. The earliest ancestors of the Norse began appearing in Scandinavia sometime after 3000 B.C., when tribes from the south and southeast began to move into areas that are now Denmark, southern Sweden, and southern Norway. Some regions had fertile plains and temperate valleys that allowed for the extensive growth in agriculture and the building of towns and villages. In much of Scandinavia, however, the new civilization clung to narrow coastal areas surrounded by mountainous terrain and harsh climates. Hunting and gathering played a more important role in the subsistence of people who settled in these places.

The early Norse displayed many of the character traits that would become associated with the later Vikings. Their customs and beliefs were clearly Germanic, including belief in a pagan religion with multiple deities who possessed many human qualities. Among the deities the Norse worshiped was Thor, the god of thunder and eldest son of Odin, the god of war and death. The importance the Vikings placed on skill and bravery in battle can be largely attributed to the high regard in which they held mythical warrior figures such as these. They also believed that those who died in battle would spend their afterlife with Odin in a great hall called Valhalla. Here they would feast with their revered god and continue to engage in battle on his behalf after being brought there by maidens called Valkyries. This was seen as a much more desirable fate than going to Niflheim, a dark and unpleasant world where the Norse believed men who died of other causes than being slain in combat were destined to go. The dread of ending

These early woodcuts depict Viking armor and weapons.

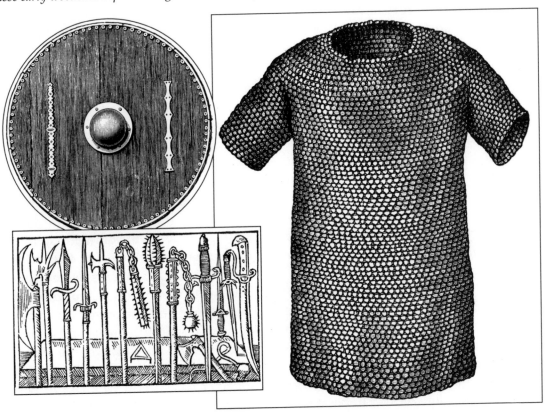

up in Niflheim also contributed to the Norse's glorification of armed combat and an honorable defeat at sword point.

ARMORERS AND CRAFTSMEN

Another important factor in Viking warfare was the great strength and quality of their weapons and tools. The Norse have come to be recognized as skilled craftspeople who created stone, bone, wood, and metal objects that were both functional and beautiful. Archaeological evidence indicates that the Scandinavian ancestors of the Norse began to display these talents very early. Among the objects discovered that date from the early settlement period are ornate pieces of jewelry, durable and practical tools, finely crafted hair combs, and early versions of snow skis and ice skates made from animal bones and leather straps.

One critical factor in the development of a distinctive Norse culture was the advent of the Iron Age. The early immigrants first used stone and then bronze in crafting heavy tools and wares, much like people in southern Europe. The metal ores needed to make bronze were not available locally in Scandinavia, so during the Bronze Age people in the north were dependent on central and western continental Europe for these essential raw materials. This subjected them to powerful cultural and economic influences from distant areas. Helen Clarke, an archaeology professor at University College in London, England, explains why the coming of the Iron Age was so important in enabling the Scandinavians to distinguish a separate cultural identity from other Europeans:

> The idea of using iron was, like the use of bronze, introduced from central Europe, but the metal itself did not need to be imported. Abundant sources of iron ore lay close at hand and easily obtainable . . . in central and southern Norway and Sweden and in Denmark. . . . At first the tools and weapons made by the early Iron Age blacksmiths were few and simple, but the skills and repertoire of the Scandinavian craftsmen increased over the centuries until their products were on a par with any made elsewhere in Europe.[3]

With iron readily available, the Norse used their crafting skills to develop strong and effective battle weapons such as double-edged swords nearly three feet in length, two-handed battle-axes, and spears for both thrusting and throwing. In addition, Norse warriors also used longbows, and from their ships would deluge a coastal or riverside area with arrows before landing and swarming ashore. For defense, iron shirts and helmets provided warriors with solid protection, as did their shields. Crafted from wooden planks, shields were rimmed and riveted with iron or bronze, making them able to withstand and defend against powerful force. Viking armies usually attacked with their men aligned in tight rows, with shields held up close together so as to provide a solid wall of cover. The Norse's metal-crafting skill also contributed to their ability to incite fear and horror among those that they encountered in combat, as they decorated their weapons and armor with complex, frightful images inspired by their warlike deities. Since it was common for the Norse, especially those who were wealthy or socially important, to be buried with their worldly possessions, many of these well-crafted weapons have been preserved and turn up in excavations of burial sites.

VIKING DEITIES

During the Viking age, the Norse in Scandinavia and elsewhere almost entirely adopted Christianity as their religion. Prior to that, the Norse had been pagans, just like other Germanic peoples. Instead of worshiping just one god, the Norse recognized many gods. Even though there are few people in the world who still follow this belief system, some of these gods have still found their ways into everyday life, for example, in the names for the days of the week.

Besides being the god of death and war, Odin was also the god of wisdom. His Old English name was Woden, and Wednesday is named for him. Along with his wife, Frigga, goddess of the clouds, Odin reigned over all the other Viking gods and goddesses.

Thor, the god of thunder, was a warrior who protected humans against giants who dwelled in the underworld. Thor was said to have a magical hammer he used to slay the giants, and the image of Thor's hammer is widespread in Viking jewelry and artwork. Thursday is named for Thor. This underworld was ruled over by Loki, a tricky, fiendish god, and his frightful daughter, Hela.

Another warlike Viking god was Tiu. Depicted in pictures with full protective armor and Norse battle weapons, Tiu had only one hand. Vikings believed he had the power to bring victory in battle. Tuesday is named after Tiu.

Frey and Freya were brother and sister. He was the god of weather and harvest, she the goddess of love and beauty. They were among the most popular Viking gods. Friday is named for Frey and Freya.

Balder was a wise, youthfully handsome, and magical god. He was gentler than the more warlike Thor and Tiu, and was also very popular among the Vikings. Known as the god of the sun, Sunday is named for him.

A Warrior Ancestry

The discovery of such weapons from the period before the Viking era is an indication that, before they turned their military efforts elsewhere in the world, the Norse engaged in frequent battles among themselves, and established a raiding and warring tradition. Archaeological evidence indicates villages and settlements in the Norse homelands were often protected by large fortifications. In some places, these structures were knocked down and rebuilt several times, indicating that attacking parties would destroy them and set them up again after gaining control of the area. The recovery of many valuable artifacts from this ancestral period has been possible largely because those who owned them buried them deeply and securely, indicating a need to protect them from raiding and plundering.

Written accounts of Norse life in the pre-Viking era are few. Those that do exist provide additional evidence of a battle tradition. These historical documents, combinations of fact and fiction, cannot be taken as absolute truth, but they contain accounts of conflict among rival Norse factions. The Icelandic historian and scholar Snorri Sturluson wrote about some of these conflicts in his work *Heimskringla,* recognized as one of the leading sources of information about the Vikings. In a section of *Heimskringla* called "The Saga of the Ynglings," Sturluson describes violence between different Norse peoples within Scandinavia that very closely resembles the activities that the Vikings would become famous for during their heyday. This passage describes a conflict between a Danish leader named Fróthi and a Swedish king named Óttar:

> Fróthi was a great warrior. One summer he proceeded to Sweden with his troops and made an incursion into it, harrying, and killing many, and making some prisoners. He collected immense spoils. He burned the villages far and wide, and ravaged the land.
>
> In the summer following King Fróthi sailed on a warlike expedition to the Baltic lands. King Óttar learned that Fróthi was not in his kingdom. Then he boarded his warships and sailed to Denmark, and there he ravaged the land without any resistance being made to him. . . . Then he harried in the Vendil District, burning, and devastating the land.[4]

A few of the *Icelandic Sagas* dealing with the early migration and the settlements of the Norse's ancestors include similar references to these kinds of attacks and conflicts between different factions, as does the Old English epic poem *Beowulf.*

"The Saga of the Ynglings" also includes descriptions of violence and slaughter resulting from power struggles within kingdoms and ruling families. One such incident occurred between two brothers, Alrek and Eirik, both of whom were Norse kings. After these two brothers had traveled together away from their kingdoms and not been heard from for a long time, a search was undertaken. The brother kings were both found dead, their heads having been bludgeoned. "They had had no weapons besides the bridle bits of their horses," says the saga, "and it was believed that they had killed each other with them."[5]

Clearly the Norse people were historically accustomed to military conflict and possessed the skill and resources to create powerful weapons of war for many centuries before they began attacking their neighbors with any great strength or frequency. This raises the question of what led the Norse to undertake the ambitious ventures, starting around the end of the eighth century, that led to the Viking era. Probably the most prominent reason was the great importance the Norse placed on possessions and valuables and the social status and prestige that came with such wealth.

WEALTH AND STATUS

The Norse custom of burying their dead with their personal possessions has provided modern archaeologists and historians with plenty of evidence to prove how important material wealth was in Norse society. Items found in graves in the Norse areas of Scandinavia include such valuables as fine silks, spices, wines, bronze and silver jewelry, and glass and ceramic pieces. These items originated in many places throughout the world, and in medieval times were usually acquired at major trading centers in Europe, Asia, and Arabia. The Norse areas of Scandinavia were a great distance from most of these trade centers, but the Norse's desire for great valuables was strong enough to motivate them to travel these distances to obtain them.

This great fondness for material wealth among the Norse was critical in determining the social and political structures they came to adapt during the Viking era, and in determining whom they came to recognize as leaders among them. Throughout the centuries leading up to the Viking era, most Norse people were farmers and herders. In many places, government or social organization was loose and informal; whoever owned the largest farm in an area or had lived the longest in a particular village might have been recognized as the leader. Some people may have had no loyalty to anyone outside their own families. In other regions, local kings and chieftains claimed command over particular areas of varying sizes.

As settled areas grew larger and Norse society became more complex, individuals, families, and villages started organizing on

Items found in graves, such as this gold collar, testify to the importance of material wealth in Viking society.

a wider scale, and some leaders were able to command more widespread loyalty and organize more powerful fighting forces. Those who were most effective in gaining this kind of following achieved success by offering the Norse the opportunity to obtain what they valued most: greater wealth and status. The exchange of wealth and riches, or at least the chance to gain them, in return for professing loyalty to a leader became the basis upon which much of Norse society organized itself at the beginning of the Viking period. This sort of relationship was recorded by the Roman historian Tacitus at the end of the first century A.D., when he visited Scandinavia and observed the people of the Svear kingdom, one of the largest and most organized Norse alliances. Tacitus said the Svear considered wealth to be of such great importance that it led them to "accept one of their number as supreme."[6] That is, the Svear chose their ruler and maintained their loyalty based on who attained the highest level of wealth.

For over two thousand years, the Norse and their predecessors were able to satisfy their desire for wealth through trade and commerce, and through raiding and plundering against their fellow Scandinavians and closest neighbors. However, after several centuries of development, Norse society became increasingly competitive. The emphasis put upon one's wealth and social status became increasingly intense, driving large numbers of people to seek wealth and status beyond what they could obtain through farming, craftwork, trading in marketplaces, and periodically raiding nearby areas.

The Norse knew their Christian neighbors kept money and valuables in churches and monasteries, believing these to be safe places immune from military attack. There was also a lack of governmental and military organization in Christian Europe at that time, and few kingdoms could provide sufficient military force to protect a sacred site against a strong attack. Knowing that there were great treasures stored in poorly defended places nearby, and not sharing the religious beliefs of their Christian neighbors, the Norse had strong incentives to launch more frequent raids in the late eighth century. With offers of loot and generous reward, young, strong Norsemen were recruited for this purpose. When Norsemen went on these missions of plunder, they described it as going "a-viking," and many historians believe this is how the Norse acquired their dreaded name. The label of Viking is therefore often reserved just for those who ventured out of their Scandinavian homelands to other places in the world.

LOOKING TO NEW LANDS FOR POWER AND FREEDOM

Because they were primarily interested in material goods, the Vikings' military activity was, for the first several decades of the Viking era, almost exclusively made up of hit-and-run raids. However, conditions in the Viking homelands eventually led to many Norse people finding the large, mostly unprotected land areas in much of Europe to be just as tempting as

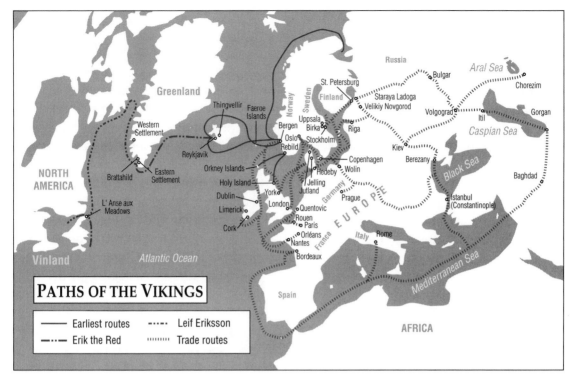

PATHS OF THE VIKINGS

Earliest routes ---- Leif Eriksson

---·-- Erik the Red ········ Trade routes

the easy wealth that was to be had there. After several years of successful, relatively easy raiding, massive amounts of wealth had accumulated in the Viking homelands, and much of this wealth ended up in the hands of the leaders. Their strength and power grew along with their seized loot, and rivalry for supremacy in the Norse homelands became a major motivating factor in the Vikings' pursuit of landholdings abroad.

Many kingdoms and chieftaincies were growing larger and taking over villages and other local affiliations. Often, those who gained power over these larger domains raised the levels of command and control they held over the lives of those they claimed as subjects. Some individual Norse found themselves being told how much land they could keep and what pro-

fessions they were permitted to pursue. Some were even required to turn over some of what they owned or acquired through their work and trading activities. Because Norse society traditionally placed great value on individual freedom, and considered personal gain and improvement of one's status highly virtuous and desirable, it was very difficult for many people to accept newly powerful rulers imposing their wills upon them. Some even came to believe that they could live a more truly Norse lifestyle by leaving their homelands and settling elsewhere. Many nearby European and British territories were either completely open or only lightly settled, with little or no military presence, making them inviting places to settle. Those Norse who sought new places to establish new Norse strongholds also followed those who went abroad to raid or make conquests for their homeland leaders.

So the Norse had reasons for their Viking attacks, they had a battling tradition, and they had the ability to create weapons and equipment well suited for battle. All the makings for the Viking age were in place except one: a means to travel the distances to places where the loot and land they sought were located. This was provided by the most historically prominent feature of their culture: Viking ships.

VIKING VESSELS: VEHICLES TO GREATNESS

From the time Germanic tribes began to settle in Scandinavia, boats were a critical part of their lives. The rugged terrain in much of Scandinavia meant that travel between villages and settlements over land was very difficult if not impossible. Travel by sea, or through inland waterways such as lakes and rivers, was much faster and more practical. The Norse developed a skill for shipbuilding that was unmatched by any society that had existed until that

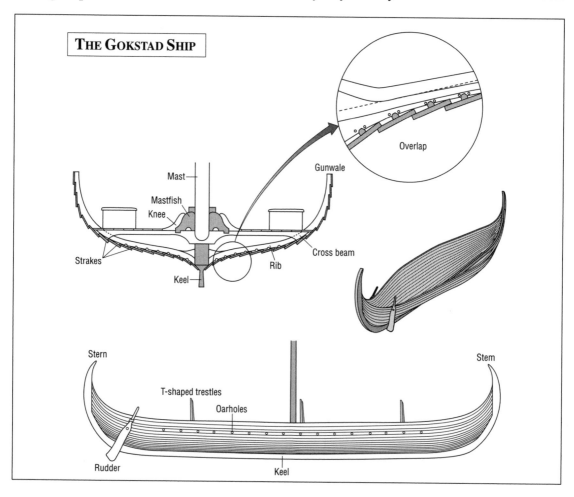

THE GOKSTAD SHIP

Overlap

Gunwale

Mast

Mastfish

Knee

Cross beam

Strakes

Rib

Keel

Stern

Stem

T-shaped trestles

Oarholes

Rudder

Keel

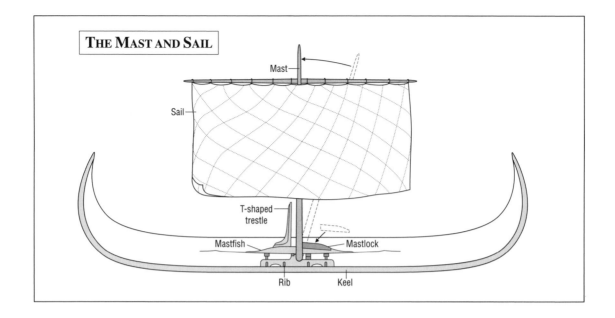

THE MAST AND SAIL

Mast

Sail

T-shaped trestle

Mastfish

Mastlock

Rib

Keel

time. Crafted from very thin overlapping planks, and usually made from sturdy woods such as oak or pine, their ships were both durable and flexible. They were long and narrow, had a shallow draught, and had a prow on both sides. Magnus Magnusson, an Icelandic Viking descendant who is one of the world's most recognized experts on the Vikings, says the Viking ship "helped make the Viking Age possible and has remained its most evocative symbol in the public's mind."[7] Their design and construction enabled them to move swiftly and smoothly in shallow seas, and also gave them great maneuverability even in narrow, shallow, rocky, and rapid inland waterways. As the Viking age commenced and increasingly large parties took to the boats for overseas ventures, the vessels grew in size to enormous proportions. The largest Viking ship of this kind ever recovered, measuring 118 feet long, was excavated in 1996 in the Roskilde fjord in Denmark. Historical records indicate that late in the Viking era, a few other ships greater than 100 feet in length were also constructed.

For a long time these vessels, known as longships, were propelled solely by oar power. Oar-powered ships were excellent for transportation within Scandinavia and were likely used by the Norse in raids against local rivals. But to travel the distances the Vikings ultimately would during the height of their power, they needed more than just oars; they also needed to harness wind power.

The first Norse sailing ships appeared around the year 700. Up until this time, these boats, cleverly crafted though they were, did not possess a keel—a sturdy structure running from the front to the back of the ship and across the full width. Once this became a regular feature, masts and sails could easily be added, and

THE VIKING SHIP MUSEUM

After archaeologists found the remains of five Viking ships in the Danish village of Skuldelev in 1962, plans were made to build a Viking ship museum in nearby Roskilde to house them. The ships found in Skuldelev and on exhibit at the museum include two warships and three cargo ships. One of the warships has been shown to have been built from Irish oak, most likely in Dublin. Replicas of some of these ships have been built and successfully sailed.

In 1996, while workers were digging during the construction of an addition to the museum, they uncannily stumbled upon the remains of nine more Viking ships. One of these was the longest Viking ship ever discovered, measuring 118 feet in length and capable of carrying one hundred people.

Norse ships became truly remarkable creations. Magnusson elaborates:

> The combination of sails and oars gave them a speed and maneuverability that took Europe totally by surprise; their shallowness of draught allowed them to penetrate rivers that gave them access to rich inland cities like London and Paris. They needed no harbors, for they were designed to be beached on any shelving sandy shore. They could land warriors and horses anywhere and everywhere, and in retreat they could reach islets in the shallow waters of estuaries that other boats could not navigate. They gave the Vikings a huge advantage over their opponents.[8]

With both oars and sails, the Vikings could travel across great ocean stretches regardless of weather conditions. The Norse used these ships not just on their raids and conquering ventures, but also for explorations far to the west of their homelands. With these ships the Norse traveled to and settled in North Atlantic islands and territories such as the Faeroes, Iceland, Greenland, and even briefly northeastern North America. Then again, their versatility and ability to move swiftly, even against the wind, made the Norse's new and improved ships ideal for venturing into shallow coastline waters and making subsequent quick escapes. In other words, they were precisely suited for Viking raids. And thanks to these unique craft, the Norse would thrust themselves upon an unsuspecting world—a world that would never be the same after their arrival.

Chapter

2 Early Invasions: Vikings Take Root in England and Ireland

The targets of the earliest Viking raids in the British Isles were like the Lindisfarne monastery—sacred Christian religious sites. For example, *The Anglo-Saxon Chronicle* recounts a Viking attack on another Northumbrian monastery in 794. Many coastal islands were easy targets because they were isolated and poorly defended. The island of Iona, located off the coast of Scotland, had a large monastery that was founded by an Irish saint in the sixth century. This monastery was raided three times between 795 and 806. Viking raids in Ireland are first recorded in 795, when monasteries on three coastal islands were attacked and plundered. For the next forty years, steady if sporadic raiding continued at monastic centers along the coast of Ireland.

In England very little raiding activity took place after the first few years of the ninth century. The Danish Vikings who conducted most of the raids there during the early part of the Viking era were more interested in the vast riches of the Frankish Empire on Europe's mainland continent. But this was to change in 835; as *The Anglo-Saxon Chronicle* reports, "In this year the heathen devastated Sheppey."[9] An island off the eastern coast of England,

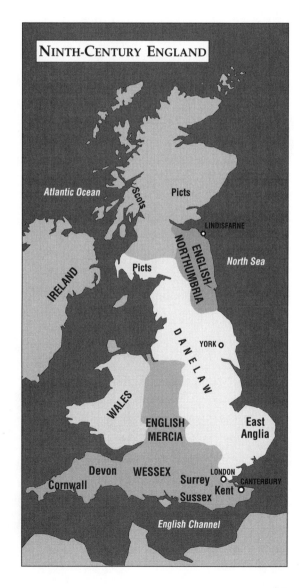

NINTH-CENTURY ENGLAND

Atlantic Ocean

Scots

Picts

LINDISFARNE

Picts

ENGLISH NORTHUMBRIA

North Sea

IRELAND

DANELAW

YORK

WALES

ENGLISH MERCIA

East Anglia

Devon

WESSEX

LONDON

Surrey

CANTERBURY

Cornwall

Kent

Sussex

English Channel

Sheppey was but the first English settlement to fall in the newest wave of incursions. The *Chronicle* then records Viking raids almost every year from then through the middle of the century.

THE LURE OF THE MONASTERIES

Both England and Ireland were thoroughly Christian. The recognition of monasteries and other important religious places as sacred sites inappropriate to be targeted for military attack was firmly rooted in the beliefs of people in these lands. England had been under Rome's rule for a while, and although certain outlying tribal peoples were never brought under control of the empire, most of Great Britain shared the benefits of being a part of the Roman Empire. Rome's military and economic strength kept peace among

Vikings warriors conduct one of many raids on the English coast.

rival factions that had historically occupied Britain, and between these tribes and the Roman settlers. Although the decline and fall of the Romans had meant renewed fighting among local kingdoms and tribal factions within England, the Christian belief system that had come with the Romans stayed strong and grew after their departure. The Romans never conquered as far as Ireland, and warfare among local factions there had been constant for several hundred years before the Vikings came. Nevertheless, Christianity had come to Ireland under the legendary missionary St. Patrick. Holy church and religious sites were deemed worthy of respect and were not often subject to attack.

The Vikings, of course, sacked the monasteries for a reason. Precious metals and other great valuables were kept at these sites, both as property of the church and as safety depositories for the highly wealthy. Although fortified against attack with high buildings and oceanfront boundaries, monasteries were not watched carefully or heavily protected by local military forces. The opportunity for quick and easy plundering was too strong a temptation, and the Vikings pillaged one coastal settlement after another.

However, the people of Britain and the other Christian areas where the Vikings attacked seemed unable to understand what attracted the Vikings to the monasteries. Since these targets were all sacred to Christian faith, the locals readily concluded that the Vikings, who were pagan after all, must be vehemently anti-Christian. The most reliable historical sources for information on the Viking raids were written by the monks who were targeted by the Vikings. They describe their adversaries in profoundly ugly terms. There is no doubt that the Vikings could be and often were ferocious and overzealous in their slaughter, and the Vikings were also known to capture slaves and hostages on their raids. Still, many historians believe that the most dramatic and dreadful descriptions are a result of the monks' partiality against those who so viciously attacked them and their misunderstanding of the Vikings' motives. These descriptions are often mixed with references to omens of evil and wrathful acts of God, such as this one from the *Annals of St. Bertin*, a ninth-century chronicle kept by monks living in a monastery by that name in an area that is now in France:

> The Northmen . . . devastated all the coastal regions, plundering and burning. God in his goodness and justice, so much offended by our sins, had thus worn down the lands and kingdoms of the Christians.[10]

THE FIRST RAIDERS

Norse mythical texts that also contain references to the early Viking raids in Britain and Europe are also skewed. These are partially fantastic accounts that are intended to glorify Viking warriors, even describing them as possessing supernatural, mythical powers. So all major sources of information regarding who these Vikings were that launched the raids that started the Viking era are not totally reliable. However, through research and archaeology, historians have some idea who the early Vikings were and where they came from.

It is likely that the earliest raids in England were made by Norwegian Vikings who had settled in the smaller British islands to the north and west. But the Danes would wreak the greatest carnage in England and have the more profound impact on its culture. The raids made by the Danish Vikings were undertaken by larger fleets and were targeted more toward the south of England. It was easier for the Danes to reach this part of England from their homeland, as they could sail along the west coast of the continent and then cross the relatively narrow channel. The earliest raids in northern Britain were so few and far between, and the raiding parties so small, that it is unlikely they would have been made by Norsemen traveling so far away for so short a time across such great distances of open sea.

The raiders who visited Ireland were mostly Norwegian. It is clear that during the first years of raiding, they came largely from the Orkneys and Shetlands, islands north of Scotland where Norwegian settlers had been migrating for several years prior to the time the recorded raids began. Although there were Danes who visited Ireland (and Norwegians who raided England), the Norwegians had the largest impact on Irish civilization. Overall, the Viking presence in both Ireland and England was strong, and the culture remained on both islands well after it had faded elsewhere. While Viking power in continental Europe largely vanished by the end of the tenth century, Viking influence in Ireland and England lasted well into the eleventh century.

Norwegian raiders are shown landing in Ireland. Norwegians dramatically changed Irish civilization.

ON THE MOVE IN IRELAND

After initially limiting themselves to remote coastal areas, the Norwegian raiders in Ireland started moving inland in the 830s. One particularly famous Viking raider in Ireland was a chieftain named Turgeis. Author Peter Brent writes about Turgeis in his book *The Viking Saga:*

> No one is certain now when exactly he landed in Ireland; in his as in so many cases, legend obscures history. But he was probably of royal descent and certainly a man of vigor and ambition. . . . He made the power of the Viking felt—and felt as one of the contending powers within Ireland.[11]

These "contending powers" were heavily armed kingdoms and factions within Ireland that, at the time of the initial Viking raids, were fighting with each other frequently and intensely over supremacy of Ireland. This divisiveness prevented the Irish from effectively defending against the raiders, and Turgeis and his band of Vikings took full advantage of the situation. They pillaged the inland religious center Armagh, the most sacred site in Ireland. The *Annals of Ulster*, an ancient text that records historic events in Ireland during the medieval period, notes in the entry for 831 "the first plundering of [Armagh by Vikings], thrice in one month."[12] Turgeis continued to raid churches and other holy sites through a wide section of the Irish countryside, including Tara, the seat of Ireland's nominal high king. New Viking arrivals, equally eager to partake of the easy plunder, steadily reinforced Turgeis in his ventures.

Word of the success of these raids spread far and wide among the Norse. More raiders from the Norwegian homeland, as well as the islands close to Ireland, undertook expeditions. It was also in the 830s that the Danes began to expand their raiding activity, both on the continent and in Great Britain. The lure of easy riches in Britain and Europe was overwhelmingly powerful to opportunistic Norsemen.

EARLY VIKING SETTLEMENTS

With their new, reliable source of wealth returning such rewards, the Norsemen considered their raids to be worthy of greater resources and greater efforts. Hence around 840, after their massive marauding during the previous decade, Vikings first started taking up settlements in Ireland for the winter months between raiding seasons. Ireland's kingdom armies were heavily armed and battle tested. Once they realized the threat the Vikings presented, the Irish forces prevented them from regularly enjoying the kind of unhindered success they had initially. To protect themselves within Ireland, the Vikings built encampments known as *longphorts*, which were well fortified and had strategic access to waterway passages.

The first of these longphorts was completed around 841 at the modern capital of Dublin. Longphorts were created at other locations, such as the cities of Cork,

Limerick, Wickford, and Waterford. These military-oriented bases were not temporary installations; they attracted settlement and grew into towns with central village areas. Prior to the Vikings' arrival, there were no cities or towns in Ireland. It was strictly farms and rural land, with monasteries, churches, and fortress castles scattered throughout the countryside. The Viking longphorts were the initial settlements that developed into many of Ireland's modern towns and cities.

A passage from the *Annals of Ulster* describes how in 841, when the first longphorts appeared, the Vikings were "on Dublin still," meaning that they had remained and settled there. Further Viking activity is described:

Maelduin son of Conall, King of Calatrium, was taken prisoner by [Vikings]. The plundering of Cluain-Mic-Nois by [Vikings] from Linn-Duachail. The plundering of Biror and Saighir by [Vikings] from Dubhlinn [Dublin]. A fleet of Norsemen on the Boyne [River] . . . . Another fleet of Norsemen at Linn-sailech in Ulster.[13]

The *Annals* chart other Viking terrors throughout the next year. Clearly the Norsemen were becoming a permanent and menacing presence in Ireland.

In fact, with the establishment of the longphorts, the Vikings appear to have enjoyed dominance over the Irish for several years. Many of the Irish tribes lived as ruled subjects of the Vikings. The *Annals of*

The outline of a Viking encampment, known as a longphort, is visible in the Irish countryside.

St. Bertin includes this passage from 847: "The Irish, who had been attacked by the Northmen for a number of years, were made into regular tribute-payers. The Northmen also got control of the islands all round Ireland, and stayed there without encountering any resistance."[14] However, this unchecked success was short-lived. In the late 840s, Irish forces, acting with unusual unity under then Irish high king Malachy, drove the Vikings out of most of Ireland's countryside and into their protective longphorts. Dublin itself was invaded by the Irish in 849, and an alliance between the Irish and Danish Vikings from England drove the Norwegians out of Dublin around 850. However, a new influx of Norwegians came to Dublin in 853 and recaptured it. The new leader of the restored Dublin Vikings was called Amlaíb, or Olaf the White. He reigned for eighteen years and resumed invasions of Irish territory. He also undertook ventures in Wales and Scotland on the island of Great Britain, expanding the power of Viking Dublin to greater levels. In the wake of his death, his successor was proclaimed the king over all the Norse in Ireland as well as Great Britain. However, within Ireland itself, effective opposition to the Vikings rose again among the divided kingdoms. After Amlaíb's death the Vikings were again largely driven out of all areas but the longphorts by around 890 through the joint efforts of various Irish factions.

However, the Vikings in Ireland still found other ways to make their presence felt, even if their territories were less secure. With typical practicality, they exploited the divisive conditions within Ireland, making alliances with various warring factions, always with the aim to further their own goals. This led to a considerable degree of social interaction and integration between the Norse and the native Irish. After their attempts to take land were rebuffed, many Vikings turned their attention to crafts and trade instead. Many also married into the local population and either left the longphorts or brought their new Irish families in to live with them. As a result, many of the original Viking settlements in Ireland lost their unique Norse character. Among those Vikings that did maintain their cultural identity, many focused whatever militarist efforts they made into fighting on behalf of their local Irish allies.

The Vikings of Dublin remained militant and autonomous from the surrounding country, but even they were unable to gain and hold much territory outside Dublin. Eventually anti-Viking sentiment among the Irish grew to the point where their strongholds came under increasingly harsh attack. By 902, the Viking position in Ireland had become so weakened that a combined force of Irish from the nearby kingdoms of Brega and Leinster drove the Viking rulers out of Dublin altogether, burning and destroying the city. The *Annals of Ulster* record that the Vikings "left a great number of their ships and escaped half dead, after having been wounded and broken."[15]

The longphorts did not enable the Vikings to gain over Ireland the kind of dominance they had over other, smaller British islands. However, they did create areas within which the Norse could settle solidly and establish themselves. Some

Alfred the Great and the Burned Cake Loaves

Famous for reviving English unity and putting up stiff opposition to the Viking invaders, King Alfred the Great is also the subject of a tale concerning a cowherder's wife that has become a part of English folklore.

According to the tale, the king came to a peasant cottage dressed as a hunter and asked for shelter. The woman who greeted him did not recognize the king—at that time he had fled to the deep marshes in the kingdom of Wessex to escape the Danish Vikings. However, the woman, whose husband was herding cattle at the time, allowed the king to enter and sit by the fire under the condition that he watch the cake loaves she was baking.

The king agreed, but when the woman returned, the cakes had burned. The peasant woman scolded the king sternly, all the while unaware of his identity. This story is most likely fanciful, but nevertheless a good indication of how renowned Alfred was for his gentle manner and sensitivity toward his subjects. In spite of these character traits, he was still a determined fighter who earned recognition in much of the world for his effective opposition to Viking forces on his native soil.

Norse who migrated to the longphort areas became integral parts of the local communities. The early establishment and success of the longphorts did enable the Vikings to maintain a relatively long-term presence in Ireland. They would return there in the following century, taking a different, more successful approach toward settling and establishing themselves among the native inhabitants.

Vikings Settle in England

Vikings voyaging to England did not start staying for the winter until ten years later than their counterparts in Ireland. Furthermore, unlike the Viking settlers in Ireland, the earliest Norse inhabitants of the settlements in England showed no interest in conquest and territorial gain. Instead, the Danish Vikings who came to England set up settlements on wide uninhabited areas on offshore islands, using these settlements as bases from which to raid English targets. Although they stayed longer than the Vikings who had come during the first half of the ninth century, the Vikings who stayed over in England at midcentury did not stay for good. The settlements facilitated their raids, but those who remained there usually did so for only one year.

The Vikings' motives took a definite turn in 865, when the "Great Army" arrived in Britain. *The Anglo-Saxon Chronicle* describes this army as "a great heathen host,"[16] and unlike other hostile Viking forces seen before in England, this one wanted to settle itself on the mainland. Numbering in the thousands, the Great Army was led by seasoned warriors named Ivar the Boneless, Hálfdan, and Ubbi, all of whom were probably of Norwegian origin. The army consisted of many fighting elite from the most powerful Danish kingdoms, but it did not come representing any of the major leaders in Scandinavia. The members of the Great Army acted on their own behalf, taking loot and territory for themselves and displacing the native inhabitants on the lands they were occupying.

The arrival of the Great Army truly marked a dramatic change in the significance of the Vikings in Great Britain. No longer simply a threat to coastal monasteries and sacred sites containing riches, the Vikings now sought to take control of the kingdoms in which they had been raiding. Their attacks became massed and concentrated. Towns, villages, castles, homes—anyone or anything that the Great Army came across was a potential target.

While England was, like Ireland, divided into several smaller kingdoms, the separate English kingdoms were mostly at peace with each other and did not possess the kind of large, well-armed, and battle-seasoned standing armies that the Irish did. Largely for that reason, the Great Viking Army fared far better in England than did the Vikings based in the longphorts of Ireland. The Vikings in England quickly conquered large sections of the huge island. The city of York in Northumbria fell to the Vikings in 867. *The Anglo-Saxon Chronicle* notes that "immense slaughter was made of the Northumbrians, . . . and the remnant made peace with the host."[17] Thereafter the Vikings pushed into the rest of Northumbria, the kingdom of East Anglia, and part of the central kingdom of Mercia in short order.

Once established, the army used its secure landholdings to launch continued raids and attacks, plundering and confiscating every kind of valuable and terrorizing the English people. Although they usually did not fight battles with mounted cavalry, large Viking armies like this one did capture horses and use them to transport themselves over land on raids and attacks. This enabled the Vikings to broaden their frontiers of conquest. The kingdoms of East Anglia and Northumbria were both conquered, and their kings were executed by the Vikings. There are different accounts of how they were put to death, but they are all equally ruthless and gruesome. By one account they were tied to trees and shot with arrows until they died, but most historians now believe they were more likely slaughtered by a Viking technique called blood eagle. In this form of execution, the victim's ribcage is broken open along his spine, and his lungs are pulled out, so his corpse resembles an eagle with "bloody wings" sprouting from his back.

DANES AND ENGLISH LIVING TOGETHER

Soon after the Great Army's arrival, only one major English kingdom, Wessex in the southwest, remained under English control. King Alfred, who came to power in 870, ruled Wessex and proved to be a much better strategist than the other English kings. Soon to be known as Alfred the Great, this monarch had proven himself battle worthy in the previous year fighting alongside his father and predecessor against Viking invasion. After fighting nine battles with the Vikings during the first year of his reign and holding his ground, Alfred came to terms with them. He made no challenge to the areas they had conquered in return for being left in peace. Initially intended as a temporary truce, this agreement was later strengthened to give full formal control of much of northern and eastern England to the Vikings. This area became known as the Danelaw, and its foundation was very important in both Viking history and the history of Great Britain.

Within the Danelaw the Vikings settled permanently, taking up farming and herding. *The Anglo-Saxon Chronicle* records that in 876 "[Viking leader] Hálfdan shared out the lands of Northumbria, and they [the Vikings] were engaged in ploughing and making a living for themselves."[18] Later on, many people from royal and ruling families in Denmark came to the Danelaw, some bringing their followers, to set up new kingdoms and principalities over which they asserted their rule. Like the longphorts in Ireland, the Danelaw in

Alfred the Great, King of Wessex, came to terms with the Vikings.

England solidified and stabilized a Norse presence. But the Danelaw covered a much larger area than the longphorts, and the reduction in hostilities brought about by the agreement with King Alfred gave the Vikings in the Danelaw time to settle peacefully.

Probably the most important development within the Danelaw was the rise of some of the most thriving and global trade activity seen in western Europe until that time. People from throughout Europe and the Viking settlements in the North Atlantic came there to meet and do commerce. The city of York especially became a bustling commercial center. Although

York's history as a town and trading center dated back to the Roman era, under Viking occupation it grew significantly and gained great importance. Magnus Magnusson discusses the Viking impact upon York in his book *Vikings!:*

> Under Viking rule, York doubled in size. It became the largest trading city in Britain, with an estimated population of some 30,000, and one of the most important mercantile cities in western Europe—the main Scandinavian trade outlet outside of the British Isles. . . . By the year 1000, according to a Life of St. Oswald, "York was enriched with the treasures of merchants who came from all quarters, particularly from the Danish people."[19]

"BLACK AND WHITE" VIKINGS

Vikings came from Denmark, Sweden, and Norway, but usually the people in the areas to which they came made no distinction between them, simply calling all Norse people Vikings. The Irish were an exception. When Danish Vikings started to arrive in Ireland shortly after 850, the Irish began differentiating between them and the Norwegian Vikings who were already there. The Irish called the Danes "black Vikings" and the Norwegians "white" or "fair" Vikings. This was probably because the Danes were less likely than the Norwegians to have blond hair.

The *Irish Annals* describe the battle between the Danes and Norwegians for the town of Dublin in 851: "The coming of Black Foreigners [Vikings] to Ath-claith [Dublin] who made a great slaughter of the White Foreigners; and they plundered the fortress, between people and property. The entry for the following year includes this passage: A fleet of eight score ships of White Gentiles [Vikings] came to fight against the Black Gentiles. . . . They were three days and three nights fighting; but the Black Gentiles were successful, "that the others left their ships with them."

There are additional references to both black and white Vikings in the *Annals,* but only one more entry that describes them fighting with each other. Other accounts of the two Viking groups describe conflicts taking place between them and various native Irish factions. This indicates the degree to which Ireland was fragmented during that time in history, and how the Vikings, once they were established in Ireland, became embroiled in the complex power struggles there.

The spoils of the trade wealth that arose in the Viking areas resulted in quality living among both the Viking immigrants and the local people, among whom the Vikings mingled and integrated. The overall result was a strong, affluent area in England under Viking control, where people from many places in the world visited, lived, and thrived. The society the Vikings created in the Danelaw was, by fair historic measures, a definite success.

However, the agreement establishing the Danelaw did not keep Viking attacks at bay for long. *The Anglo-Saxon Chronicle* reports that a Viking king named Guthrum launched an attack from Cambridge upon Wessex in 878. Guthrum's forces "rode over Wessex and occupied it, and drove a great part of its inhabitants overseas, and reduced the greater part of the rest to submission."[20] King Alfred himself escaped to a secluded fortress surrounded by swampy marshland, from where he sent messages throughout the country, rallying forces to fight a guerrilla war against the Vikings. After raising a large enough army to meet Guthrum head on, Alfred defeated him decisively in the Battle of Edington. The Vikings left Wessex and agreed to remain within their own territories. Another interesting concession the Vikings had to make was to embrace Christianity. As Vikings were to do so often in so much of the world, the Vikings in Wessex did this readily and with no apparent reservation. This willingness to embrace Christianity when their worldly and political goals could be met was characteristically Viking and expressly contradicts the notion that the Viking raiders were motivated by anti-Christian sentiment.

The English did not completely cease action against the Vikings, either. Starting in the early tenth century, lands within the Danelaw were recaptured by English armies led by the successors of King Alfred, who had put great effort into raising strong forces to oppose the Vikings. But the Danelaw was securely a Viking area for long enough that the influence and impact of the Vikings' presence there remained important for centuries to come. Ironically, the success of the Danelaw and the quality society created by its Danish Viking rulers seems to have inspired the people who would one day come to conquer them—the Vikings of Norwegian origin who were driven out of Ireland.

VIKINGS RETURN TO IRELAND

When the Norwegian Vikings were driven from Dublin, many fled to areas in England under control of their fellow Norse. During this time they regrouped and reinforced, and after a while again attacked Ireland, beginning with a massive raid against the old Viking stronghold of Waterford in 915. Later they overcame opposition from combined northern and southern Irish forces and reoccupied an area near the old Dublin in 917. Here they founded a new town with the same name. The overall situation in Ireland had remained unstable, with none of the local kingdoms or factions achieving supreme power within the country. The Vikings reestablished themselves in many of the

VIKINGS IN SCOTLAND

In addition to England and Ireland, the Vikings also established themselves in Scotland. There is considerably less information about their presence and activities there, but that which exists suggests a markedly different kind of experience for the Vikings in Scotland.

Although sites in Scotland, especially in the northern and western coastal islands, were among those attacked in the earliest Viking raids in Britain, overall the Vikings who came to Scotland were far more peaceful than those who came to England or Ireland. There was widespread settlement of Norse people on both the Scottish coastal islands and the mainland, but these settlements were mostly rural in nature, having developed in areas where few if any people of the local population dwelled. As a result, the Vikings in Scotland had less need for violent confrontation in pursuit of their goals.

Among those whom the Vikings did encounter in Scotland and elsewhere in their North Atlantic voyages were Celtic monks. However, these monks were hermits who had migrated from the monastic centers; they did not possess the vast riches typical of the monks there, and the Vikings were not incited to attack them. A tribal society known as the Picts also inhabited some of the Scottish areas where the Vikings settled, but there is no indication that there was large-scale violence between them. In fact, there appears to have been a rapid and extensive assimilation between the two groups. The Picts adapted many of the Vikings' more advanced farming, crafting, and building methods. On the other hand, the Vikings, as they did in many other places, readily converted to Christianity, which the Picts had been taught by Irish missionaries. Anthropologists consider the Scottish cultural identity that emerged in the ensuing years to be an amalgamation of the Celtic, Pict, and Norse influences that converged in Scotland during the Viking age.

longphorts, where they could possibly draw support from people with Norse roots from earlier Viking settlement. Once their power was rebuilt, the Vikings not only turned to conquest but also established vibrant commercial centers that produced wealth and stability to both Norse settlers and local populations. At this time the Vikings were expanding territorially throughout the world, especially in the North Atlantic. With their geographic setting adjacent to the European continent, the other British islands, and the western Viking settlements in the Atlantic, the Viking centers in Ireland were well positioned to reap the benefits of the widely expanded world trade fostered by the Viking presence.

The Vikings reestablished themselves as a major force in Ireland. Along with the strength gained by the success of their new urban trade settlements, they were also bolstered by new strategic alliances with local Irish factions. Although the *Annals of Ulster* describe Viking battle activity during the tenth century, it is mostly in the service of their Irish allies against other local tribes. The Vikings did not spend extensive time and effort in pursuing great territorial gains for themselves, as they had previously done in Ireland. Hence the Vikings gained enough of a footing to maintain their presence in Ireland while at the same time strengthening themselves by expanding their power elsewhere in Britain.

It was the pursuit of power elsewhere that led the Vikings of Dublin to launch ventures in Great Britain immediately after regaining their Irish base. Dublin's King Ragnold had asserted dominance over the Isle of Man just to the west of Great Britain and had also made territorial gains in Wales, Scotland, and northwest England before capturing the kingdom of York from the Danish in 919.

The defeat of York's Danish Vikings by Norwegians from Ireland signaled a growing complexity in the situation in the British islands. The nature of the Viking presence in both England and Ireland had changed, as did the relationships between the Vikings and the native peoples. Clear-cut divisions and lines of conflict between Viking raiders and invaders and English and Irish rulers and inhabitants were becoming less distinctive. Local populations had become significantly mixed ethnically, and people's loyalties and preferences among warring factions were not so easily determined. Confusing matters further, the Norse in Britain were showing signs of the internecine rivalry that had been going on in their homelands for many years, and were not always united in their efforts against the English and Irish. Sometimes they even formed alliances with local factions that brought them into conflict with each other. The Vikings continued to be the main perpetrators of conflict in the British islands for more than another century, but it was no longer possible to examine conflicts in England and Ireland strictly in terms of the Vikings versus the Irish or English.

Chapter

3 Viking Rule: A Dublin Dynasty and Danish Kings of England

The conquest of York by the Irish Vikings was not the dawn of a new era of dominance for them in England. King Alfred the Great, probably realizing he faced the threat of an overall Viking takeover of Britain, had devoted himself to rebuilding his military forces. He and his successors were able to gradually regain control over much of the land held by the Vikings through the late ninth and early tenth centuries.

Upon gaining the throne of York, Ragnold immediately recognized the rule of the English king over all the territories he held, including those he had won back from the Danish Vikings since the start of the tenth century. But this was not a successful appeasement. In 927 English king Aethelstan defeated Viking king Olaf to recapture York for the English. After being driven from there, the Vikings made a concentrated effort to recapture York from the English during the 930s, with large numbers of Vikings from many different factions combining their efforts. But these forces were likewise defeated decisively by Aethelstan when they met in the Battle of Brunahburh in 937. *The Anglo-Saxon Chronicle* graphically describes the triumph of the English forces:

There lay many a warrior

Of the men of the North, torn by spears,

Shot o'er his shield.[21]

Aethelstan led a large, well-organized, disciplined, and strongly armed force. When confronted with this kind of opposition, the Vikings often did not fare well in conflicts, and the fact that such a force had been mustered in Britain after a century and a half of Viking incursions was one of many factors that changed the overall situation in Britain starting in the early tenth century. Another factor was the degree to which the Norse had become integrated into the British population after many years of settlement and conquest. There were many people of mixed heritage by this time, and interaction between those of native British and Norse origin was widespread and common. Allegiances between rival factions were not so clearly defined in strict terms of British versus Viking, as many people of partial or full native background sometimes found themselves quite happy under Viking rule.

Relationships between different Viking contingents, and the political and social situations existing in their homelands, were also changing at this time. Before the Vikings from Ireland drove the Danes out of York, there had been some conflict between these two groups, but it was minor and infrequent. Back in Scandinavia, consolidation of power was progressing to the point where single central rulers were on their way to gaining total control over what are now the nations of Denmark and Norway. These powerful rulers had larger forces and more resources than previous Norse rulers, and were starting to show a desire for widespread territorial conquests

The Jomsvikings

"Every Summer they went out and made war in different countries, got high renown, and were looked on as the greatest warriors; hardly any others were thought their equal at the time."

This quote from the "Jomsviking Saga" refers to a group of warrior Vikings who attained semilegendary status during the Viking era. The Jomsvikings were one of several *Viking-unions* or *Viking-laws.* These were independent, mercenary forces who quite often ended up in the service of Danish kings. The union had its own rules. Only men between the ages of eighteen and fifty could join. The warriors were required to live peacefully with one another within the fortress, and avenge attacks against their fellow warriors as if they were blood brothers. To show fear in any situation or retreat in the face of an enemy of equal strength was forbidden. Women were barred from entering the fortress, and neither women nor children could be taken prisoner. Any loot the Jomsvikings plundered was put into a pool to be shared evenly among them. Any violation of rules resulted in immediate ejection from the Jomsvikings.

The Jomsvikings were supposedly based in the Danish fortress of Jomsborg. While the date of their origin, if in fact they existed, is uncertain, it is generally considered to be around the year 980. This raises the question of just how long the Jomsvikings were around. Some of the Vikings hired by the English king Ethelred after the attacks in the early eleventh century were believed to be Jomsvikings. King Magnus of Norway destroyed Jomsborg in 1043, and most historians believe by that time the Jomsvikings had already disbanded. Although their history was a short one, the Jomsvikings did make a big name for themselves in the annals of Viking history and legend.

and even far-flung empires. They were also feeling pressure from each other over who was to be dominant within Scandinavia itself. Harold Fairhair had united much of Norway under his rule, and major kings and leaders elsewhere in Scandinavia were competing with him for dominance in the homelands. Many of the Vikings who came to Britain during the second half of the Viking era were members of fighting forces loyal to these rulers who sought to bolster their positions and better their fortunes. Along with them were members of the armies and contingents who had suffered defeat in the internecine Scandinavian battles, and those who sought to avoid the imposition of control over their lives by the newly powerful rulers. They all came in search of new places to plunder, conquer, settle, and inhabit.

All these circumstances set the stage for the next century and a half in Great Britain and Ireland, when conflict between various Norse and native factions intensified, and power and influence over widespread areas fluctuated frequently.

DUBLIN AT THE PEAK OF POWER

The Irish Vikings did finally regain control over York in 939, but their rule only lasted fifteen years, and there were no more Viking kings of York after that. The fall of Erik Bloodaxe, the last Viking king of York in 954, is considered an important turning point in the history of the Dublin Vikings in Britain. At that time the Dublin Vikings had attained a substantial level of affluence, having rebuilt their network of longphorts in Ireland and gearing these power centers toward open, widespread trade instead of military venturism. Avoiding deep involvement in Irish civil conflict, the Vikings focused on fostering the greatest possible wealth for themselves and the native populations in the areas they occupied.

This new activity in Ireland coincided with the widespread growth of Viking settlement throughout Europe and the North Atlantic. The Viking trade center network in Ireland benefited greatly from being geographically and strategically able to facilitate trade among the far-flung Viking settlements. This brought new energy and prosperity to the areas in Ireland under Viking control, and gained them a following among many native Irish, especially in areas where the Norse and natives had coexisted for a long time. The Vikings again entered into warring alliances with Irish factions, this time establishing steadier, longer-lasting partnerships than they had previously. The most notable of these alliances was the one between the Vikings of Dublin and the southeast Irish kingdom of Leinster. This helped the Vikings to avoid creating too much nationalistic backlash against them among the native Irish.

At the peak of their power, the Vikings of Dublin effectively ruled not only their areas of settlement in Ireland and York, but also the Western Scottish Islands and Orkney Islands where early Norse settlers had migrated, and an area in England known as the Five Boroughs that by treaty belonged to whoever controlled York. The death of Erik Bloodaxe did mark the last time there was an officially recognized Viking king of York, and the Orkneys and other islands effectively became colonies of the growing Norwegian territorial alliance, but the Irish Vikings' power endured at least within and around their settlements. Indeed, if the Vikings could have completely avoided involvement with the ongoing Irish civil conflicts, they may have kept control over parts of Ireland for longer than they did. However, the practical military alliances they entered into did not allow for this.

DUBLIN'S DECLINE

The kingdom of Leinster was embattled in the internal power struggles of Ireland, especially with an increasingly powerful sovereign named Brian Boru. Boru was claiming the right to rule all of Ireland and gaining substantially in his efforts to assert that claim. The Vikings were drawn into the conflict through their alliance with Leinster and consequently went to battle against Boru's forces. This resulted in Viking forces suffering a major defeat in the Battle of Glenn Máma in 999, after which Boru entered Dublin and occupied it. Glenn Máma was the last nail in the coffin of Viking conquest. Prior to this, the Vikings had been largely eliminated from effectively controlling any territory much beyond Dublin by another Irish king, Mael Sechnaill, who defeated them in the Battle of Tara in 980. The *Annals of Ulster* describes the event:

A great slaughter of the [Vikings] was committed, and their power banished from Ireland. . . . Ragnall, son of Amlaimh, King of the [Vikings], and Conamhal, son of a [Viking] chief, and many others, were slain.[22]

Historians agree this passage is overdramatic. The Battle of Tara probably did put an end to whatever remaining Viking military venturism was still going on, but at this time that venturism was not large. The absorption of the Vikings into the Irish population, their concentration on establishing vital commercial centers, and their alliances with local Irish kings had already done much to minimize an overt Viking presence, especially a violent one.

THE VIKINGS LINGER

After their defeats at Glenn Máma and Tara, the Viking rulers in Dublin were allowed to remain in power, and the Norse people who had settled in the other Viking areas were not driven out. The great trade prosperity brought by the Viking presence apparently worked in their favor, as their Irish foes, while not wanting the Vikings to gain control of their homeland, did recognize that the invaders possessed strengths and characteristics that could benefit their own people. Besides thriving trade, the Vikings also produced ships and navigational aids for the Irish that greatly enhanced their seafaring abilities; for the first time Ireland had merchant ships and fishing fleets. Clearly, having the Vikings around

BRIAN BORU: IRISH HERO, VIKING FOE

Like England's King Alfred the Great, Ireland's Brian Boru became renowned for his effective opposition to the Viking invaders in his country. As a young man Boru used to hide outside the Viking city of Limerick and ambush those who ventured from its protective limits. When he grew older, he drew a large enough following to be able to conquer the Limerick Vikings and also become king of Muenster, a large kingdom in the southwest of Ireland. This was the beginning of Boru's rise to power, which would lead him to become ruler over all of Ireland.

Boru achieved this feat after the Battle of Glenn Máma in 999, when he defeated the Dublin Vikings and Irish forces of the kingdom of Leinster, who had risen up in revolt against his rule. With this opposition put down, Boru was able to demand and receive support from his chief rival in the north of Ireland, King Malachy of Meath. In 1004 he toured the entire island, proclaiming himself to be high king and receiving no challenge. Never before in Irish history had one ruler been able to assert control over the whole country.

Although his forces were decisively victorious against the recurrently rebellious Leinster Irish and their Viking allies at the Battle of Clontarf, Boru himself did not survive the battle. As things turned out, the battle was fought on Good Friday, and being devoutly Christian, Boru refused to participate in warfare on such a holy day. Instead, he secluded himself in the woods near the battle site and spent the day in solemn prayer. This would prove to be his undoing.

After initially being pushed back toward the coast where their ships were docked, the foreign Vikings staged a comeback, seemingly a last desperate effort, and broke through the Irish lines. They propelled themselves forward into the woods where Boru had secluded himself. A Viking chief named Brodir from the British Isle of Man slashed off the head of the Irish king. Brodir and the other Vikings who had come upon Boru were immediately surrounded and executed, but it was too late to save the man who had brought Ireland more together than any before him. In spite of Boru's death, the Vikings and their Leinster allies were soundly defeated, and Brian Boru became legendary as a martyr for Ireland and its people in their battle with the Vikings.

provided some benefit for the local population.

The most visible though not actually most important blow against the Viking presence in Ireland came in 1014 at the Battle of Clontarf. Once again, the Vikings had no stake in the fray. This battle ensued from a personal feud stemming from an insult made by a son of Brian Boru against a Leinsterian ruler. Passions burned so strong that massive forces were mobilized by both sides in anticipation of battle. *The Annals of Ulster* says, "A valorous battle was fought between them, for which no likeness has been found. The [Vikings] and the Leinstermen were defeated . . . so that they were entirely annihilated."[23] Although the overall effect the conflict had on the Vikings' strength and presence in Ireland was marginal, it has become legendary in Irish history as the event that drove the Vikings out of Ireland. Boru, although victorious, was slain during the conflict; he was thereafter recognized as a martyr in defense of his homeland.

What was probably significant about the battle was the massive number of Viking forces mustered and the many different places and great distances from which they came. The Dublin Vikings called upon their fellows from the Norwegian settlements in the Atlantic islands, the Norwegian homeland, and possibly also from Norse-settled areas in Europe. The combined forces of Leinster and the Vikings have been estimated as high as twenty thousand, with the Vikings supplying from one-fourth to one-half that number. That so many Norse would rally around the Dublin Vikings in a battle that did not present a very serious threat to them is surprising. One possible explanation relates to the growing rivalry in Scandinavia for dominance between what were by this time the virtually united kingdoms of both Norway and Denmark. About the same time, another large army from Denmark was attacking England with the objective of full conquest of the country. Although Ireland had never lent itself well to conquest by the Vikings, perhaps the Norwegians hoped that with a massive force of their own, combined with the Leinster kingdom's, they might make permanent territorial gains in Ireland after all. A major conquest in Ireland would definitely help balance a Danish takeover of England, something that was looking increasingly likely at that time.

The Viking forces at the Battle of Clontarf were clearly the largest and most formally militarily experienced Viking forces ever gathered in Ireland. Nevertheless, the Vikings and their Irish allies were again outmatched on the battlefield. The losses suffered by their forces were great, with estimates of as many as six thousand Vikings and three thousand Leinstermen slain. The Irish nationalist forces still did not see fit to drive the remaining Vikings out of Ireland, and they made no attempt to destroy their stronghold in Dublin, as they had over a century earlier. In fact, the king of Dublin at that time, Sigtrygg Silkybeard, was allowed to continue his reign for the rest of his life, about twenty more years. However, the extent of the Viking military losses in the Battle of Clontarf probably did discourage any fu-

Foes meet at the battle of Clontarf, described as the event which drove the Vikings out of Ireland.

ture plans for a major Norse assault on Ireland.

By the late eleventh century, the Vikings were no longer politically or militarily significant in Ireland, and prominent signs of Norse culture and lifestyle had largely disappeared. However, the Vikings had achieved greater success in Ireland during the tenth century than in the previous one. By focusing mainly on trade and the creation of prosperity, relying mostly on alliances with local Irish factions to provide for their military needs, and extensively mixing with and integrating into the native population, they brought greater wealth to Ireland, brought it into wider contact with the rest of the world, and developed several vital urban centers that were to have lasting significance.

A Viking Revival in England

At least initially, the resurgence of Viking power and influence in Ireland in the early tenth century coincided with a definite decline of Viking power in England. After Erik Bloodaxe was deposed from York, it may have seemed that Viking power and influence in England would even end completely. The English had slowly but steadily built up effective military forces in response to the Viking threat, and these forces had enjoyed great success beginning in the early tenth century. However, over the twenty-five years following the Viking loss of York, the native British once again seem to have lost resolve, and their military preparedness underwent serious decline.

Much of the blame for the reversion to weakness by the native English is given to King Ethelred, who ascended the English throne in 978 and became known as "Ethelred the Unready." Norse raids against the English resumed in 980 and continued over the next three decades, increasing in size and intensity. There were no longer powerful fighting forces in England to defend against these attacks, and the Vikings once again exploited this lack of military strength and leadership to further their pursuit of riches and power.

Beginning in the 990s, these raids were led mostly by two Norse leaders whose forces were far more militarily organized and disciplined than the early raiding parties and the first invading army in England. One of these leaders was Olaf Tryggvason, who had been raised in the Viking city of Novgorod, located in what is present-day Russia. Although he was Norwegian, his fleet of ships, which numbered near one hundred, was most likely manned by Swedes. Swedish Vikings were most common in the eastern European territories, and this was probably the first time a large Swedish contingent had joined an attack upon England. "The Saga of Olaf Tryggvason" in *Heimskringla* indicates he began his raiding rampage in continental Europe, then "sailed to England, harrying far and wide in that land."[24] The saga continues to describe raiding ventures by Tryggvason in other parts of Britain and Europe. He gained enough wealth and power from his excursions that, when he returned to his native Norway, he was able to win the throne of the kingdom in 995.

The other major leader to head up forces intent on attacking England was the Danish king Svein Forkbeard. His forces first appeared in England in 994. *The Anglo-Saxon Chronicle* depicts a force of ninety-four ships sailing into London for the purpose of burning and looting, but came under heavy siege and suffered great loss. The story continues:

> But in this the holy Mother of God manifested her clemency to the garrison and delivered them from their foes. They went away, doing as much harm as any host was capable of doing in burning, harrying, and slaughter, both along the coast and in Essex, Kent, Sussex, and Hampshire. Finally they got themselves horses, and rode far and wide wherever they pleased, and continued to do unspeakable damage.[25]

Danish king Svein Forkbeard's ships raided the coasts of England for twenty years.

This kind of activity by Forkbeard's forces continued over the next twenty years. With the full resources of the king of Denmark, which by now had essentially become a unified state under one kingdom, the ferocity and frequency of Viking-style raids throughout much of England became rampant.

DANEGELD

It was during this time, with Tryggvason's and Forkbeard's forces aggressively active, that the practice of paying *danegeld* to the Vikings came into practice. Danegelds were effectively bribes that English officials, clerics, towns and villages, or individuals paid to the Vikings to persuade them not to attack. This practice had taken place in continental Europe as early as 845, when a Frankish king had effectively bribed Viking attackers with thousands of pounds of silver, convincing them to cease their attacks against the city of Paris. In England, the first recorded payment of this kind took place as early as 865, when the people of the town of Kent exchanged payments in return for a Viking commitment not to attack them.

In 991, attempting to spare the town of Malden from attack, Viking raiders offered to refrain from their intended raid in exchange for payment by the town. However, Malden's leaders turned down the Viking request, and in response the Vikings overran the city and its English defenders. Seeing how successful the Vikings were in this attack, King Ethelred made a payment of ten thousand pounds of silver to get them to cease their aggression in England. Like most danegelds, this one accomplished the immediate goal of holding off the Vikings from attacking. However, the major Norse forces in Britain during those years only found motive to repeat their threats and offers with increasing frequency. The payments also served to encourage increasing numbers of Norse to come to Great Britain for the wealth and power that could be had there with little effort. *The Anglo-Saxon Chronicle* sums up the situation quite concisely in the entry for 1011: "And notwithstanding all this peace and truce and tribute, they went about in bands, and robbed and slew our unhappy people."[26] The danegeld payments grew larger, reaching over sixteen thousand pounds of silver in 994 and forty-eight thousand pounds in 1012.

The drain the danegelds placed upon the English authorities eventually weakened them so much that they were unable to govern effectively. People in many areas of England came to recognize Danish king Forkbeard as their sovereign, sometimes as a term of agreement with the Viking aggressors. The disarray and weakness that had paralyzed the English left no challenge to Forkbeard's claim. He was able to extract massive amounts of valuables and other commodities from much of England, and his troops and operatives had widespread freedom of movement. Nevertheless, Forkbeard seemed intent upon complete control, and he landed with the largest Norse army assembled yet in England. Magnus Magnusson offers this insight into Forkbeard's foray: "The invasion by Svein Forkbeard reflected a new pattern in Viking attitudes toward England. The attacks were no longer casual and sporadic. The armies that came over now were professional and highly organized."[27]

Using an advantage that earlier Viking forces did not have, Forkbeard marched through the country rallying Danish loyalists, who were now considerable in number after so many years of Norse migration and settlement. He overwhelmed all opposition, getting most local lords and citizens to submit without a struggle. Even among nobles and other influential citizens, many people were by now either of Norse or mixed Norse-Anglo heritage. Whatever their backgrounds, the English population at this time had good reason to follow whatever leadership was going to provide the most stability and well-being, and the current English king had not succeeded in doing that. Ethelred fled the country, taking up exile in mainland Europe, and after two

Svein Forkbeard's army was the first highly organized and professional Viking army to raid England.

hundred years of Danish incursions, Forkbeard became the first Dane to rule as king of England in 1014.

BUILDING A VIKING EMPIRE

Forkbeard may have had many motives for launching his invasion even though he was already so favorably positioned in England. Supposedly, English king Ethelred had convinced some of Forkbeard's most valued warriors and commanders to stay on in his service after an especially strong attack against the English in 1012. Ethelred had also enraged Forkbeard some years earlier when, as part of a campaign to eliminate

people of Danish heritage from the English population, he had Forkbeard's own sister, who was living in England, slain. On the other hand, Forkbeard may have had reasons to establish stronger control over England that were not so personal. His army landed in England about the same time that the large alliance of Norse forces dominated by Norwegians was converging in Ireland. Norway was consolidating power over both its own territory within its own borders and many of the settlements created by Norwegian explorers and conquerors over the previous two centuries. The Danish ruler may have felt himself being challenged by the emerging Norwegian power

CANUTE, VIKING EMPEROR

He was fully Danish and the son of a Viking conqueror of England, yet Canute is recognized for having a largely peaceful reign as an English king and winning the love and respect of the English people. After skirmishing briefly with former king Ethelred and his son Edmund, Canute did not engage in hostile conflict within England, and in fact had little need to. However, things were not so peaceful for Canute back in his native Scandinavia.

Canute's brother Harald had been holding the throne in Denmark since Canute had accompanied his father on his voyage of conquest to England. Then, in 1019, Harald died. Canute immediately returned to Denmark to defend the throne against internal challengers to the Danish throne. Later, Canute fought Norwegian king Ólaf Haraldsson, defeating him and adding Norway to his empire in 1028. According to English chronicler Henry of Huntingdon, when Canute died in 1035 he was "lord of the whole of Denmark, England and Norway, as also of Scotland." This is recognized as the largest empire ever attained by any Viking ruler.

To gain power over an empire that size, Canute had to be very much a traditional Viking warrior and conqueror. He may have been considered peaceful within England, but elsewhere he acted much the same as his Viking predecessors.

for dominance among the Norse kingdoms, and the placement of massive military forces in England at that time may have had strategic implications. Considering the events that followed, this last possibility seems more likely.

Forkbeard was only the first of a succession of Danish kings to reign over England. Following his death in 1014, Forkbeard's son Canute claimed the throne. Canute had to defeat a force loyal to the deposed Ethelred led by his son, Edmund Ironside,

who was deemed the heir to the throne by the English upon Ethelred's death. Following that, Canute and Edmund fought until reaching agreement on a divided rule of England. This agreement is described in *The Anglo-Saxon Chronicle*:

Both kings met at Alney, near Deerhurst, and became comrades and sworn brothers, and made a compact both with pledge and also with oaths, . . . and then dispersed, King Edmund to hold Wessex and [Canute] the country to the north.[28]

However, this divided rule lasted only about one year. Upon the death of Edmund a short time afterward, Canute was recognized by all parties as the king of all England.

Following this, Canute assured his control over the nation of Denmark and defeated King Haraldsson of Norway, putting that country under his rule as well. He gained extensive territory in Sweden and was accepted as ruler by Scotland and the northern Atlantic islands with an allegiance to Norway. Canute ruled the largest empire ever headed by a Viking or person of Norse descent, but he was dramatically different from the people who had come to be known as Vikings in the ninth century. This king over both Denmark and England was a royal warrior, not an adventurous young man looking to gain some quick loot or find new, distant lands to settle. In fact, Canute resided mostly in England and is buried there alongside other kings, and during his reign he maintained widespread peace within England. Except for some outlying coastal areas, England was not harried by Viking raids or other Viking attacks during his reign. Much more integration of Danes and other Norse within England also took place, and the nobility in England came to include many more people of Danish heritage. The distinctions between Viking outsiders and native English, already fading, became even less pronounced during Canute's reign.

A Controversial Coronation

After Canute's death his sons, Harefoot and Harathnacut, ruled as kings of their father's empire until 1042. After this the next two kings of England were natives. The first was King Edward, known as Edward the Confessor, who reigned until 1066. Upon his death, his brother-in-law, Harold Godwinsson, took the throne of England. This was a very controversial move on the part of Harold, based on actions he had taken in the years prior to his assuming the throne.

Godwinsson was one of many people living in England at that time, among both the ruling class and the commoners, who were part Danish. One of Godwinsson's grandfathers was a Viking who had settled in England. Perhaps it was that part of his heritage that led him to engage in some of the activities attributed to him during the reign of his predecessor. These included raids against Ireland and other western British islands, and even participating in a minor revolt against Edward that was staged by Harold's father, Earl Godwin, in 1051. This taste for venturism may have sprung from his Viking roots, but was not why his coronation was controversial. That controversy resulted from a meeting he had two years earlier with another European ruler and the discussion they supposedly had in which Godwinsson agreed not to claim the English throne for himself but instead support the other ruler as the next claimant to the English throne.

Godwinsson was one of three major historic figures to play a role in events in

1066 that would prove to be monumental in world history and be seen as signifying the end of the Viking era. The European leader he met with was Duke William of Normandy, who would become known as William the Conqueror. William was another of the major figures to play a role in the events of 1066. His power and prestige arose from Viking activity in western continental Europe, activity that proved to be at least as dramatic, destructive, and ultimately important to world history as the Viking ventures in Britain.

4 Heights of Fury: Vikings in Frankia and the Western Continent

The same pattern of Viking activity that occurred in Britain—initial raiding that increased in frequency and intensity, followed by large-scale occupation, conquest, and settlement—also occurred in western continental Europe. Many of the same conditions that existed in Britain that prompted Viking attacks also existed in that section of Europe. However, there were also some differences that ultimately made the area even more attractive for the Norse adventurers.

Like England, most of western continental Europe had been a part of the Roman Empire and experienced the same decline in political and social stability after its fall. However, there was a large section that had benefited from being the central district of another empire, the Frankish Empire. Named for the original state of Frankia, which consisted of territory mostly in what is today France, it became stronger and more stable than any other western European kingdom since the end of the Roman era. Hence Frankia and much of the surrounding area did not experience the same level of governmental, social, and military disarray that England had during the centuries leading up to the Viking period. There were also not numer-

ous heavily armed and battle-seasoned rival factions within Frankia as there were in Ireland, at least not at the beginning of the Viking age.

CHARLEMAGNE AND THE FRANKS

The state of Frankia was already larger and more powerful than any other in western Europe when, in 771, King Charlemagne—Charles the Great—took over its throne. One of the most charismatic and celebrated leaders in history, Charlemagne expanded his empire to include territories to the south, east, and north of his initial holdings. By the year 800, Charlemagne and the Franks were so powerful that the pope declared Charlemagne to be "emperor of the Romans." In fact the territory that Charlemagne controlled was not nearly as big as that held by the Romans during the height of their empire, and some of the territories held by the Franks had never been under Rome's control. The instatement of Charlemagne as a new Roman emperor was largely symbolic, but it was an indication of just how powerful he and the state of Frankia had become in Europe. A large portion of the material wealth generated during the Roman Empire lay within the boundaries of Frankish territory and was effectively under Frankish control and protection. Furthermore, the stability created by the powerful rule of Charlemagne provided a safe environment for active trade and commerce, and this generated even greater wealth in those areas. Like the rest of Europe that had been under Roman control, Frankia was thoroughly Christian, and monasteries and other religious sites were

recognized as sacred places, considered safe from attack. As a result, large amounts of wealth and valuable items were kept in these locations, just as they were in Great Britain and Ireland.

The Norse people were familiar with the vast wealth of the Frankish Empire. They traded there themselves at major commerce centers, civilly and without aggression, during the years leading up to the Viking era. Pressures from competition within the Scandinavian homelands for power had not yet reached their peak, so the incentive for the Vikings to raid and pillage was not great. The power of Emperor Charlemagne and the fighting forces he commanded were also likely a reason why the Vikings did not attack Frankia aggressively until well into the ninth century. An account recorded by a monk at the Abbey of St. Gallen in Switzerland indicates that the Norse may have known of Charlemagne and been intimidated by him, but the information is suspect. According to the story, in the year he was decreed Roman emperor, he was in a town on the Mediterranean Sea, enjoying a meal, when ships were sighted coming toward the shore. Charlemagne immediately recognized them as enemies, and the monk who wrote the account indicates that they were Norse. Actually, Islamic Moors were much more likely to be plundering in the

A statue at a monastery in Switzerland depicts the powerful emperor Charlamagne.

Mediterranean at that time. Whatever the identity of the raiders, the monk implies that Charlemagne's mere presence in the area was enough to scare them away:

> When the Northmen heard that Charles was there, they vanished in marvelously swift flight. Rising from his table, the most just and devout [Charlemagne] stood looking from the window, while his tears ran down and no one dared speak to him. Then he explained his tears to his nobles in these words: "I do not fear that these worthless scamps will do any harm to me. No, I am sad at heart thinking that while I live they dare intrude upon the shore, and I am torn by a great sorrow foreseeing what evil they will do to my descendants."[29]

Most likely this passage was written sometime after the massive Viking attacks on Frankia had commenced. The intention may have been to make Charlemagne look good in predicting the future and recognizing the coming threat. Regardless of the story's accuracy, it is true that during Charlemagne's reign, the Vikings made little threat to the Frankish Empire.

FIRST IN FRISIA

Although the Franks possessed a formidable army, it would be incorrect to assume there were no Viking incidents or attacks during Charlemagne's rule. The first recorded raids on Frankish territories occurred about the same time as those on Great Britain and Ireland. In 799

a Viking raid was recorded in the Vendée region along the northern Frankish coast. There was an attack on the coastal region of Frisia, an area particularly rich and active in trade, in 810. The Vikings who raided in this northern Frankish territory were mostly Danish, and the coastal areas they attacked were within easy reach from their homeland. They were also relatively remote and not well defended. Frisia was a very active commercial trading area, and the concentrations of riches to be found there provided strong incentive for Norse raiders. Some Norwegian Vikings were also among those plundering the Frankish coast. Operating out of the British Islands, these Norwegians were actually able to set up a camp on the island of Noirmoutier, a good distance to the south along the coast of what is now France. Nevertheless Frankish forces stopped an attempted raid by Vikings on Frisia in 820. For more than a decade after this, Viking raids were few and limited to islands off the Frisian coast.

By this time, significant changes were under way in Frankia. Charlemagne died in 814. His son and successor, Louis the Pious, further enlarged the empire and initially maintained stability within it. But eventually Louis's own sons began to rebel against him, and other nobles and local leaders who had been loyal to Charlemagne also turned on the king. This led to instability within the empire and divisiveness among its military forces. Without a strong governing power, the Frankish Empire was at greater risk of being subjected to Viking raids and conquests.

RAGNAR LODBROK

Many Viking heroes gained semimythical status. One such hero was Ragnar Lodbrok, who was the subject of so many tales taking place in so many different locations that all of them could almost certainly not be true. He is widely associated with the Ragnar who led the first Viking attack against Paris in 845.

The name Lodbrok means "hairy britches." Legend claims that Ragnar earned that name when he crossed a moat filled with poisonous snakes to claim in marriage a Swedish princess named Thora. To prevent the snakes from biting him, Ragnar wore animal skins, with the hair on the outside and covered with protective pitch.

The places Lodbrok was said to have traveled included Finland, Russia, and Ireland as well as the western European areas that are now France. More is known about Viking warriors who are supposed to have been sons of Lodbrok, and their ventures probably helped bolster Lodbrok's own legend. These sons include Björn Ironside, the Viking who attacked Paris in the 850s and raided in Spain, Italy, and North Africa, and the leaders of the Great Army in England, Ivar the Boneless, Ubbi, and Hálfdan.

Hence raiding activity in Frisia increased dramatically in the 830s. The *Annals of St. Bertin*, which focus on historic activity in Frankia during the ninth and tenth centuries, describes the Viking attacks on the northern coast:

> A fleet of Danes came to Frisia and laid waste to a part of it. From there, they came through Utrecht [in modern Holland] to the [trading place] called Dorestad and destroyed everything. They slaughtered some people, took others away, and burned the surrounding region.[30]

Dorestad, a major trading center in Frisia located at the mouth of the Rhine River, was raided again every year through 837, with much of the town burned and destroyed each time. With the Frankish military declining into disarray, the Vikings met with no opposition, and they found the Frisian region so attractive a target that they set up a base on Walcheren, an island off the northwest coast, from which to conduct further raids. After this a large, strongly armed army led by Louis the Pious himself arrived in Frisia. Unwilling to stand up to this force, the Vikings did not make much of a showing. In this case they did not even bother to fight, but immediately withdrew from their base and ceased raiding in that area upon the army's arrival. The ease with which the Vikings could obtain vast wealth in Frisia had been eliminated, prompting their departure, but in fact Viking activity in Frankish territory had only just begun.

Once again, establishing settlements on unpopulated, remote coastal locations proved to be a wise strategy. The base at Noirmoutier had remained undisturbed since its establishment. A monastery had originally been on the island and had even remained there after the Vikings had come, but after a violent raid in 836 the monks left Noirmoutier for good. The island became a year-round base for one of three new major Viking forces to emerge in Frankia just when, fortuitously for them, Louis the Pious was dying. The Frankish Empire was plunging into full-scale civil war and was ripe for invasion. Janet L. Nelson, a medieval history professor, sums up the situation: "The wealth of the Franks had increased, along with Danish familiarity with that wealth and Danish desire and capacity to lay hands on it, while the Frankish empire's ability to defend its wealth had diminished. This was a critical conjuncture."[31]

Indeed it was, and the Vikings seized the advantage.

THE DECIMATION OF THE FRANKS

From Noirmoutier the Vikings built a large force dubbed the Army of the Loire. Another major Viking force to emerge during this time was the Army of the Somme, which based itself on Walcheren, the island upon which the Vikings previously had a base. The Danish Vikings who had been raiding in Frisia had regained control of Walcheren by entering into a strategic alliance with Lothar, one of Louis's feuding sons. This agreement is described in the *Annals of St. Bertin:*

> Lothar, to secure the services of Harald, who along with other Danish pirates had for some years been imposing many sufferings on Frisia and the other coastal regions of the Christians, now granted him Walcheren and the neighbouring regions as a benefice.[32]

Frisia became a mostly Danish-occupied area for the next several decades, with various Viking leaders given territorial concessions there. The third large force of Vikings to come to Frankia at this time was the Army of the Seine, arriving on a huge fleet that sailed up that river and occupied territory that it subsequently used as base areas for major raiding and pillaging.

These were all substantial forces, but like the Great Army that invaded England in the mid–ninth century, they were not acting on behalf of any powerful kingdoms in the homelands. These were Norsemen with raiding and warrior experience who had quite likely been in the service of Viking kings or chieftains, but now the members of these armies were pursuing their own fortunes. The base at Walcheren, for example, had been ceded to an exiled Danish leader named Harald, and the other Viking armies in Frankia also likely included many people who

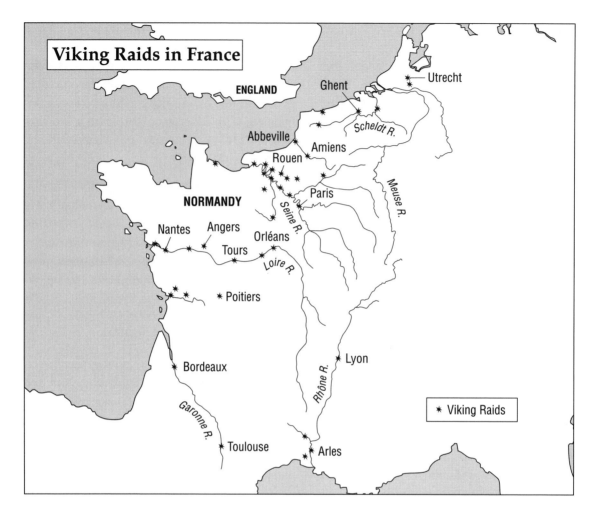

Viking Raids in France

had been pressured out of their home-lands by the consolidation of power and the greater control being asserted by the rulers there. In this way these armies were very much like the Great Army in England, and in fact some who came to Frankia with these forces later went to England and helped form the Great Army.

The establishment of these three sub-stantial Viking forces within the heart of Frankish territory was complemented by smaller Viking bands in other major river basins and valleys, all determined to lay claim to as much of Frankia's vast wealth as they could. None of these Viking contin-gents established an area like the Danelaw in England or the Irish longphorts. That is, there were no places under stable Norse control where both native and Norse might peacefully coexist. In contrast, the story of the Vikings in Frankia tends much more exclusively toward overt aggression, adversarial relations with local popula-tions, and an emphasis on destruction and looting.

The Spread of Savagery

The Frankish civil war lasted for three years, during which time the Vikings entered into alliances with the warring factions, like the one between Lothar and the Vikings of the Somme. These alliances formed by the Vikings were geared toward gaining wealth for themselves and strengthening their strategic position; there is no indication that any of the Viking forces in Frankia had a true preference among the warring Frankish parties. Occasionally, different Viking groups ended up skirmishing if their immediate objectives happened to clash—the Seine and Loire Vikings encountered each other as each became involved on an opposite side in a conflict between western Frankia and its rival neighbor Brittany. However, there were few if any significant conflicts between the major Viking forces in Frankia after the civil war was over.

The Frankish Vikings engaged in extensive raiding and plundering of not just holy sites but also villages, farms, and homes. This was especially true of the Seine and Loire Vikings, who perhaps wreaked the greatest savagery of all during the Viking age. When the civil war ended in 843, Viking raiding activity was not slowed, but instead further expanded, as the reunited Franks could not immediately organize effective opposition to the huge Viking forces amassed on their soil. In 845 the Franks were stunned to find that the Vikings had advanced so far along the Seine that they had reached the gates of Paris, one of Frankia's major cities.

The Perils of Paying for Peace

In a move that was to start a trend, Charles the Bald, who had gotten control over what is now France in the agreement that ended the Frankish civil war, got the Vikings to refrain from attacking and plundering Paris by offering them payment of over seven thousand pounds of silver. The *Annals of St. Bertin* directly calls this payment "a bribe" by which Charles "restrained them [the Vikings] from advancing further and persuaded them to go away."[33] This was the first recorded incident of a danegeld payment being made to deter a Viking attack. Following the payment to save Paris, danegeld payments became rampant in Frankia. Neil Price, an archaeologist with Uppsala University in Sweden who has researched the Vikings extensively, describes the degree to which this practice escalated:

> According to the continental sources, the danegeld payments made by the Franks during the ninth century amounted to around twelve tons of silver, most of it in cash: seven million silver pennies was paid in protection money to the Vikings over a period when the estimated total output of the Frankish mints was fifty million coins. Even without reckoning the supplies of grain, livestock, produce, wine, cider, horses, and other commodities frequently demanded in addition to the payments of bullion, that sum was equivalent to 14 percent of the entire monetary

output of the western empire for most of the century.[34]

Just as in England though, the payments in exchange for peace resulted in ever-greater threats and demands by the Vikings, whose primary objective was the acquisition of the most possible wealth for the least effort. Sadly, the efforts to purchase peace rarely pacified the Vikings for long; raiding and pillaging were constant and devastating long after large danegelds started being paid out. Towns, villages, and monasteries were ravaged repeatedly, and in addition to plundered and extorted loot, the Vikings also demanded and received ransom payments for captured Frankish nobles, clergy, and regular citizens. The wholesale destruction wrought by the Vikings was described vividly by a Noirmoutier monk named Ermentarius:

> Everywhere Christ's people are the victims of massacres, burnings and plunder. . . . The Vikings overrun all that lies before them, and none can withstand them. They seize the cities of Bordeaux, Périgeux, Limoges, Angoulême, and Toulouse. Angers, Tours, and Orléans are made deserts; the ashes of many a saint are carried away. . . .

> Ships past counting voyage up the Seine, and throughout the entire region evil grows strong. Rouen is invaded, sacked and set on fire; Paris, Beauvais, and Meaux are taken, the fortress at Melun is laid waste, Chartres occupied, Evreux and Bayeux looted, and every town invested [besieged].[35]

THE RAMPAGE THROUGH WESTERN EUROPE

The severe Viking ravaging in western continental Europe was not confined to Frankia. The Noirmoutier base was used by the Vikings to launch raids against Brittany, a region to the west of Frankia. The major Breton city of Nantes saw horrible slaughter in 843 when Vikings killed all the priests at the cathedral there, as well as many other citizens. For several decades thereafter, Brittany was subject to the same levels of plunder and violence as witnessed in Frankia. In 886 a huge number of Vikings from the Seine region joined the fight in Brittany, and together with those from Noirmoutier were able to conquer and hold Nantes and its surrounding territory. For a period of about twenty-five years in the tenth century, Vikings conquered and controlled all of Brittany.

Some other noteworthy Viking activity to occur in western Europe outside of Frankia was led by Björn Ironside, a Seine Viking who took a contingent of more than sixty ships raiding and warring through Spain to North Africa, and then along the Mediterranean to southern France and Italy. Ironside and his men captured slaves, looted towns, burned mosques (Muslim holy sites), held a Spanish prince for ransom, and engaged in sea battles. Some of the farthest reaches of Viking raiding and plundering were attained by the forces of Björn Ironside.

Ironside's ventures became legendary, but the heaviest and most devastating

LEGENDARY VIKING RAID ON LUNA

When Björn Ironside went on his famous raiding expedition to southern Europe and the Mediterranean, he went with another Viking leader named Hastein, who is the subject of a legendary story himself. As with many Viking legends, just how much truth if any there is to this story is questionable, but it does portray how clever and resourceful the Vikings could be.

After raiding and plundering in Spain, Morocco, and southern France with Ironside, Hastein's Viking brigade headed to Italy. Coming upon the town of Luna, the Vikings believed they had happened upon the city of Rome, the capital of the once mighty Roman Empire. The Vikings could not resist the opportunity to raid such a famous and illustrious city, but securely locked gates blocked their entrance. So the Vikings sent a message to the town leaders, saying that their chieftain had become sick during a storm, and he wished to convert to Christianity and receive sacraments before his death. A priest came out to administer the sacraments.

The next day the Vikings told the townspeople that their chieftain had died, and they wanted to provide him with a proper Christian burial. The Vikings were granted entry, and they brought their leader Hastein into the town sealed in a coffin and marched in procession formation around him. Once they reached the cemetery, Hastein leaped out of the coffin, very much alive and well, and fully armed. The Vikings sprang into action, raiding and plundering in a manner true to their worst reputation. Upon learning that they had made a mistake, and were not in Rome after all, Hastein is said to have set the town on fire.

Such antics were typical of the Vikings in western continental Europe during the ninth and tenth centuries. Even if there was no truth to this story, those familiar with the Vikings and the havoc they could wreak would have little trouble believing it.

Viking attacks on the western continent were concentrated closer to the areas occupied by the three major forces in Frankia. Ironside was also a major figure in those ventures, leading the second Viking attack against Paris in the late 850s, when he sacked and burned nearly all the churches in the city. This was part of a Viking campaign called the "Great Invasion," which consisted mostly of vast resurgent Viking activity on the Seine and Loire Rivers. New bases were established on two inland islands on the Seine, and the whole valley was subject to a new level of unrelenting and seemingly unstoppable Viking fury for nearly a decade following the sack of Paris. Once again the targets of attack included cities far inland, including Tours, Orleans, and Blois. With the Frankish authorities still weak and disorganized, the Vikings were mostly unhindered in their rampaging, and they ventured far from the river basins, using horses like the Great Army in England did, to transport themselves overland.

It may have been the hopelessness of the situation that finally moved Frankia's King Charles the Bald to take effective defensive measures against the Vikings. Like Alfred the Great in England, Charles had to confront the possibility that his country would be totally overrun. He built new fortresses along major rivers that could block the passage of Viking fleets. This consisted of refurbishing fortress walls and other protec-

Vikings attack Paris in the late 850s, sacking the city and burning most of the churches.

tions from the Roman period that had fallen into disrepair, and building bridges with armed garrisons along the Loire and Seine Rivers to protect major cities from future attacks. *The Annals of St. Bertin* entry for 866 tells of Charles marching to the town of Pîtres "with workmen and carts to complete the fortifications, so that the Northmen might not ever again be able to get up the Seine beyond that point."[36] Denying the Viking fleets from usage of inland waterways was an especially effective measure. Charles also needed to resort to other measures, such as continued danegeld payments, at least until the new fortifications were built up enough and adequate forces raised to provide solid protection.

The powerful leadership finally shown by Charles the Bald and the military force he was eventually able to muster were effective enough against the Vikings that many of them decided to give up their ventures in Frankia, at least for a while. It was at this time that many of the Vikings who had been active in Frankia joined the Great Army that invaded England in 867.

ANOTHER WAVE OF VIKING ATTACKS

When the Vikings turned their attention away from Frankia and toward Britain on a large scale, it gave the Franks a respite of about twenty years. They did rebuild their military forces during this time, but internal conflict among regional leaders once again caused divisiveness and insta-

Charles the Bald drove the Vikings from Frankish territory in the 860s.

bility in Frankia. Viking attacks resumed around 880, once again beginning as coastal raids against monasteries and sacred sites, then escalating. Another large fleet entered the Rhine River and captured towns and cities at a furious rate, including the Frankish Royal Palace in the city of Aachen. This area was particularly vulnerable at this time, as it was not protected by the new fortifications constructed by Charles the Bald in the western territories. The land concessions that had been made to Vikings in Frisia had kept the area relatively quiet compared with the western territories. Viking activity had been mostly contained to the coastal areas, but they now ventured boldly and aggressively inland. Vikings also made their way up the Seine River once more, and

CHARLEMAGNE AND HIS HEIRS

Throughout the Viking era in Frankia, the level of Viking involvement and success there was largely dependent upon who was in charge of the empire.

Charlemagne, by his very presence, probably discouraged heavy Viking raiding in Frankia during his reign, and he also organized effective defenses of the coastal areas. His immediate successor, Louis the Pious, benefited from Charlemagne's legacy and accomplishments, at least at first. But Louis's sons began to actively oppose him in the late 830s. That and other internal Frankish conflicts created instability within Frankia, and this led the Vikings to greater and more frequent raids and attacks. Louis did lead a large army to drive the Vikings out of Frisia in 837, but this was to be the last hurrah for Franks against Vikings for a long time.

Once Louis died and the Frankish civil war broke out, the Vikings had virtually free rein to run roughshod over Frankish territory. Even after the war was settled, the Viking menace remained fierce for several years. Most of the worst Viking activity took place in the western territories under the control of Charles the Bald. Because the Vikings did not target Charles himself or demonstrate a desire to take control of any of his territory, some historians have suggested that Charles may not have been aware of the terrible havoc the Vikings were causing in Frankia. Clearly for many years he took little or no action against the Vikings. When in the 860s he finally did, he actually achieved a great deal of success, driving the Vikings out of areas they had been freely occupying, raiding, and collecting danegelds for about a quarter century.

Charles the Fat succeeded Charles the Bald as ruler in western Frankia. The new ruler was able to use the fortifications Charles the Bald had built and the fighting forces he had strengthened to stop the Vikings from succeeding in their third attack against Paris in the 880s. This Frankish triumph made it especially clear that the days of weak Frankish resistance and defense against the Vikings were at an end, even if the Frankish Empire would never again be as strong as it was under Charlemagne.

for the third time in less than a half-century, they stood perched to attack the city of Paris in November 885.

The battle that ensued is often described as one of the most dramatic of the Viking period. Historic records say the invading forces included seven hundred ships and forty thousand Vikings, but this is likely an exaggeration. Commanded by a leader named Siegfried, these Vikings sought access to the rich territory of Burgundy, located to the south and west of Paris. The Franks' new protections and restored military forces presented a formidable obstacle to the Vikings when they reached Paris. However, Charles the Fat, who had succeeded Charles the Bald in 884, was traveling in Italy at that time and could not direct the defense of the city. With the king away, the Vikings approached the bishop of Paris with a proposition: They would spare the city if given free passage up the river to Burgundy. The bishop refused, and the battle began. The Vikings catapulted massive stones at the city walls to force their way into the city. However, they were stopped by burning oil and pitch spewed from the walls that still stood. After two days of attacks, the Vikings withdrew, having failed to overrun the city. Setting in for a long siege, they assembled massive battering rams and rock-heaving devices to overpower the barriers. The Vikings resumed their attacks in January and February. Again they were counterattacked with burning oil and pitch, but the Vikings also used fire this time, setting ships ablaze and sailing them into the city's fortifications. Still Paris held out.

A flood in February washed out one of the bridges across the Seine, and consequently some of the Viking fleet gained passage through the city. Towns in Burgundy were promptly ravaged, but the defense of Paris held. For several months the conflict remained a standoff. Finally in August, Charles the Fat arrived with a fully armed and battle-ready army, just in time to thwart a fierce new Viking offensive. The Vikings were driven back from Paris. Although some bands of Vikings made subsequent attacks, they never again threatened the city so seriously.

The Viking onslaught was further deterred in 887, with two new skillful military leaders, King Odo in the west and King Arnulf in the east, coming to power in Frankia. The Vikings were once again confronted with formidable and organized fighting forces with strong local loyalties. By 890, the Seine Vikings had been driven out of that river valley by King Odo. Viking forces in the Rhine also found their previously easy targets were becoming reinforced and that their attacks against Frankish sites would be repaid in kind. Many Vikings again found it preferable to leave instead of trying to fight against such opposition. The remnants of the Viking forces in Frankia were soundly defeated by King Arnulf and his troops in the Battle of Louvain in 891. The period of especially horrible Viking attacks on Frankish territory that had persisted for over half a century ended with this defeat.

LOTS OF LOOT BUT NO TRADE OR SETTLEMENT

The three large Viking armies operating from the Loire, Seine, and Somme were responsible for the vast bulk of violence and plunder on the western continent. While some of these same Norsemen would later join the Great Army in England, there were some traits the Vikings in Frankia did not share with those in England. These included the tendency of those in England to settle occupied lands, cultivate crops and cattle, develop thriving trade activity within the territories under their control, and blend into the local native populations of those areas.

The one place in western continental Europe that probably had the best chance to develop in such a way during the ninth century was Frisia. The agreements between the Vikings and Franks had allowed the Norse to occupy and settle there with relative peace. However, even here the Vikings were not focused on anything much beyond raiding and establishing a military presence. Those who had been granted control over the Walcheren base did not develop settlement and trade or become socially integrated with the Frisians; instead, they, like their counterparts in the other major Viking armies, were drawn by plunder. When confronted with a determined and powerful Frankish force during the early days of the reign of Charles the Fat, the Norse were driven out of Frisia, just as they had been in the Seine and Loire valleys. In his book *The Viking Saga,* author Peter Brent describes the strategy Charles used to reclaim the region. After having the most recent Viking ruler of Frisia assassinated, Charles turned his attention to thoroughly ridding the area of any Viking threat. Brent writes,

Leaderless and perhaps softened by the expectation of easy triumphs, the Danes could put

no effective force into the field when Charles chose to come at them. . . . In this way the Vikings lost their hold on Frisia, a territory which might have been their own, a Norse kingdom stretching into the Netherlands, but

Charles the Fat, with a determined and powerful Frankish army, drove the Vikings out of Frisia.

which through greed and ineptitude they had now thrown away forever.[37]

Indeed, looking at conditions in western continental Europe at the end of the ninth century, one might say Brent's description of the opportunity the Vikings had wasted in Frisia could apply equally to any of the areas they had occupied in that region. There were no areas similar to the Danelaw or Dublin and the other Irish longphort cities. In fact, the high level of violence and destruction wrought by the Vikings in Frankia actually discouraged trade and prosperity, and these areas had seen good levels of each when they were under Frankish control. Also, because they were always engaged in such hostile behavior toward the native population, the Vikings did not integrate into that population the way they did in England and Ireland. Although they had been large in number, powerful in arms, far-reaching in their ventures, and present for a prolonged period, it appeared that the Vikings in western continental Europe might not have the lasting impact that Vikings elsewhere did. As it turned out, the final chapter of the Viking story on the western continent had not yet been written.

Chapter

5 Normandy: Viking Conquest at Its Best

The expulsion of the Vikings from Frankia only lasted a few years. Around 900, a Viking fleet once again sailed into the Seine. This fleet was notably smaller than those that had previously scourged the Seine valley, and the number and scale of their attacks were not nearly so terrifying. Nevertheless, the arrival of this fleet in Frankia heralded one of the greatest, if not the greatest, ventures undertaken by Norse forces during the Viking era—the founding of Normandy, a place that would prove to be of immense importance in the coming years and centuries.

The Franks had good reason to worry over the arrival of the new Viking contingent. The recent Viking raids into Frankia had been disastrous for the Franks, and any Viking presence was certainly not welcome. The Franks may have taken some comfort when the newly arrived Norse initially took up settlements around the mouth of the Seine, and did not show the tendency toward all-out mayhem that their predecessors did. Still, the Vikings did raid in and around the Seine valley once they had a foothold. Eventually they encountered Frankish forces, and some fierce fighting erupted. Recent archaeological findings from the Seine valley at-

test to this. Many Viking swords and other battle gear items have been recovered, indicating the Vikings had come prepared for war.

It is likely, however, that these Vikings were more interested in territorial holdings on the European mainland than most earlier Vikings, given the effort they made to first establish settlements, then engage in carefully measured battles to try to obtain more. Most previous Viking venturers in Frankia had clear, strong preferences for plundering wealth rather than for trying to take and hold land.

ROLLO COMES TO NORMANDY

These new Vikings were mostly Danish but were led by a Norwegian named Hrolfur. He has come to be known more commonly by his Frankish name, Rollo, and he is historically famous for being the founder of Normandy. Information about the settlement and early history of Normandy is especially scarce; there are no known Frankish historical chronicles that were being kept during those years. The *Heimskringla* has an account of the son of a Norwegian earl named Ganger-Hrólf that resembles some of what is known about Rollo's life. According to the "Saga of Harald Fairhair," "Hrólf was a great Viking. He was of such great size that no horse could bear him, so he always journeyed on foot."[38] The saga further states that Hrólf angered Fairhair, the Norwegian king, by raiding within that country after returning from raids in the Baltic Sea. Fairhair banished Hrólf from Norway, and Hrólf set out to find a new home:

> Ganger-Hrólf then sailed west to the Hebrides, and from there west [south] to Valland [France] where he harried

---

FAMILY FEUD

When King Harald Fairhair of Norway banished Rollo from his kingdom, Rollo's mother, whose name was Hild, pleaded with the king to change his mind. Fairhair refused, and Hild warned him that it was a decision he would regret. According to "The Saga of Harald Fairhair" in the *Heimskringla* (as translated by Lee M. Hollander) Hild issued Fairhair this warning:

> "'Tis ill, giant wolf, to be wolfish,
>
> warrior, such wolf opposing.
>
> Hard that wolf will harry
>
> your herds, once he runs to the forest.

Hild was telling Fairhair that by treating her son like an outlaw and forcing him into exile, he was assuring that Rollo would in fact act like an outlaw and commit vengeance against the king in outlaw fashion.

Rollo himself never did take vengeance against Fairhair, at least not according to any historical records. However, there was continued conflict between the two families. Hild's husband was Rognvald, earl of Moer. Around the year 870 he was killed by two of Fairhair's sons, Hálfdan and Gunroth, who set his house on fire. Earl Einar, Rognvald's son and a half-brother of Rollo, avenged his father's death by slaying Hálfdan in the Orkney Islands in Britain.

Feuding between different royal families, and even between members of the same family, is depicted in the *Icelandic Sagas* as common among the Norse both before and during the Viking age.

and conquered a great earldom which he peopled to a large extent with Norwegians, and it was later called Normandy.[39]

The name Normandy derives from Norman, the Frankish word for Vikings or Norsemen. The first settlers in Normandy appear to have been successful warriors. Although the Frankish forces were still about as strong as when they had driven out the other Viking armies at the end of the tenth century, the Normans held out against them. Try as they might, the Franks could not drive them out of their initial stronghold. However, the Frankish military had regained considerable strength, the Frankish people were resolved to resist renewed Viking incursions, and the fortifications built by Charles the Bald remained formidable. Rollo's Vikings were thereby prevented from penetrating deeply inland or a significant distance from the Seine. After years of conflict, the Norse and Franks stood at a stalemate.

THE BIRTH OF NORMANDY

Rollo's Vikings made a bold move in the year 911, when they attacked the city of Chartres, a good distance inland to the south of Paris. The Franks turned back their attack, driving them back into the stronghold they had established around the city of Rouen. But following this, Charles the Simple, who had succeeded Charles the Fat as king of western Frankia, decided to take another approach toward dealing with Rollo's forces. Knowing it was

difficult to dislodge the Vikings, and that their presence had prevented other Viking groups from venturing into the Seine, he allowed them to stay where they had settled. In the year 911, Charles reached an agreement with the Norse leader Rollo that led to the establishment of Normandy. The specific size and location of the territories granted to the Norse in this agreement are not clear. Later Norman historians discuss the treaty and provide various descriptions. For example, *The Annals of Flodoard*, written later in the tenth century, speaks of "maritime [districts] with the city of Rouen which they had almost destroyed and others dependent upon it."[40] Modern historians have used a combination of evidence to conclude the original Normandy consisted of an area of roughly four hundred square miles that included the lower Seine and additional territory to the north and west. In return for the cessation of territory, the Vikings agreed to stop their attacks on Frankish soil and to continue protecting the Seine against incursions by other Vikings. Also, just as Alfred the Great had required the Vikings in England to convert to Christianity in exchange for ceding territory, Charles did the same with Rollo. Once again, a prominent Viking showed little inclination to resist this conversion when the trade-off was a major strategic gain. However, the immediate conversion to Christianity did not mean the Viking inclination for antics and rambunctiousness was eliminated. Dudo of St. Quentin, an eleventh-century Norman chronicler, recorded an incident at the signing of the treaty. Frankish bishops present at the signing said that the granting of the Norman territories was such a generous gesture that Rollo ought to "bend down and kiss the King's foot." The account continues:

> Rollo said "Never will I bend my knees to anyone else's knees, nor will I kiss anyone's foot." But impelled by the entreaties of the Franks he or-

dered a certain soldier to kiss the King's foot; and he immediately took hold of the King's foot, lifted it up to his mouth and, still standing, kissed it, thus toppling the King over.[41]

Clearly these first settlers were typically spirited Vikings, distinctive from and still hostile toward their new Frank neighbors. But the Normans and their society would undergo extraordinary change and growth in the years immediately following.

The Norwegian Viking Rollo is considered by historians to be the founder of Normandy.

NORMANS IN TRANSITION

Having an area secured for them on continental Europe, the Vikings proceeded to develop a society much like the one they had in northern and eastern England, where they were also officially granted the right to territory by a native ruler. Free of the need to devote great effort and resources to military defense and combat, the new settlers parceled out land among themselves to farm and herd. They also engaged in trade with the local European populations and with Norse people spread throughout much of the world. But unlike their counterparts in York, the Normans did not maintain a distinctive Norse or Viking culture. Instead, they fairly quickly adapted the ways of their continental European neighbors.

The Normans continued a strong tradition of art and craft creation, becoming renowned for their tapestries, architecture, and paintings. But the Normans rapidly developed a distinctive style of their own that much more resembled that of their new neighbors than it did traditional Norse styles. They developed a highly renowned style of architecture that drew heavily on European models. Perhaps the most telling indication of how much and how quickly the Normans moved away from their Scandinavian roots was the loss of their native language. Rollo's son and successor, William Longsword, had to have his son receive Danish language lessons in a more recently settled area of Normandy called Bayeux. This indicates that Danish was no longer spoken in the Norman capital of Rouen. It is perhaps even more remarkable considering that William's need for lessons came within only two generations of the settlement's founding. The assimilation of the earliest Normans into mainstream European culture and their adaptation of mainland European ways had indeed been rapid and extensive.

At the same time, there were new arrivals in Normandy from throughout the Norse homelands and Viking settlements, and many of the immigrants maintained the Norse lifestyles, customs, and traditions after their arrival. This resulted in a division within Normandy between those who had adapted to the local European culture and those who maintained their Norse origins. The Normans also seem to have absorbed under their dominion two other armies of Norse or mixed origin that had located in the coastal regions to the west of their original settlement. This meant that parts of Normandy continued to be essentially Norse in character well into the tenth century, even as those who ruled became increasingly indistinguishable from their new continental neighbors.

One Viking ethic none of the Normans seemed to abandon was that which placed high value on a wealthy, socially prestigious lifestyle. They also continued to show an inclination toward reaping additional territorial and financial gains on

Durham Cathedral in England shows that Norman architecture more closely resembled that of their new European neighbors than it did the traditional Norse styles.

the continent. Normandy thrived and prospered without the distraction of active opposition on the part of the Franks, and the Normans were able to strengthen themselves militarily as a result of their own success and the lack of Frankish interference. Although he kept his promise to protect Frankia against attacks by other Vikings, Rollo benefited from the influx of new Norse who did not yet see fit to abandon the Viking lifestyle, and Rollo either could not or did not stop them from raiding. Around 920 Normans resumed raiding activity in Frankia, and in 924 their territorial holdings grew as a result of another agreement with the Frankish authorities, this one expanding the area under Norman control by ceding them additional areas to the south and west of the original settlement that nearly doubled its size. Rollo handed over power to his son and heir, William Longsword, in 927, shortly before his death. Longsword continued to expand the holdings of the Normans, focusing on capturing Cotentin, a peninsula even farther to the west that also extended to the north along the coast of the English Channel. This area was soon conquered and ceded officially to the Normans in 933.

By not moving too aggressively or violently, the Normans did not stir strong opposition from the Franks, although there was some fighting between them in the 920s. Other factors contributed to the Normans' success in establishing and expanding their province. The fortifications the Franks had built to protect their river valleys were a good distance inland, and many of those Franks who dwelled closer to the coast abandoned those areas for the greater security to be found beyond the fortifications. Also, as long as the Normans kept more aggressive Vikings away, and only advanced themselves relatively slowly, the Frankish authorities had good reason to believe they were not worth a lot of time and effort. During this time there were other threats to contend with. As was frequently the case, there was civil unrest within Frankia and other external threats from both the south and the east. Although the Muslim invaders who had tried to penetrate the Frankish Empire in the south during Charlemagne's reign were not as much of a concern now, the Franks could not ignore them entirely. But the greatest threat facing the Franks at that time was the Magyars, Asian invaders who penetrated deep into Europe early in the tenth century. All these circumstances helped enable Normandy to grow and strengthen itself with little hindrance.

CULTURAL CONVERSION

In 935 Rollo's son William, in exchange for the new territorial concessions made to Normandy, reaffirmed his loyalty to the western Frankish king. At that point Normandy consisted essentially of the same area that it does today. It also started to establish itself as a major power in European affairs. The Normans developed a complex cultural identity that included distinctive accomplishments in the fields of politics and government, education, religion, and the arts.

TREACHERY AND TURMOIL IN NORMANDY

Everything did not go smoothly for Normandy after William's renewed alliance with the Frankish rulers. In 942 a count from the rival region of Flanders deposed William, leaving his son Richard, who was still a minor, as reigning duke. The Frankish ruler at that time was Louis IV, and he saw this as an opportunity to retake the territory that had been ceded to the Norse over thirty years earlier. The Franks moved back into Normandy and displayed ruthlessness against the people there much like what the Vikings had exhibited in Frankia during the previous century.

The Normans fought back, and opposition to the new Frankish incursion was especially strong among those who had recently come to Normandy from other Norse areas. The rulers of Normandy and those who had resided there longer had become more Frankish than Norse in their culture and customs, but the newer arrivals maintained Viking traditions and attitudes that made them very unwilling to endure their new mistreatment. In spite of his youth and inexperience, Richard was able to take back Normandy from the Franks, largely with the help of recently arrived Vikings.

Once the territory was again secured for the Normans, Richard had another conflict to contend with, this one between older and newer Normans. An overwhelming number of the recent arrivals had maintained their Norse traditions, and there was popular support in Normandy for reverting to the worship of Odin and Thor. Those who followed the old religion were especially strong in the campaign to oust the Franks, and felt unobliged by their commitment to Frankia, believing the Franks had already violated it. In the wake of their efforts and the debt he owed its followers, Richard considered reviving paganism in Normandy and discussed it with his nobles.

The lords of Normandy, who had become thoroughly mainstream European under the leadership of William, were strongly opposed. They convinced Richard that abandoning Christianity would be very damaging to Normandy and make it difficult to engage in alliances and prosperous trade with their mainland European neighbors. Normandy remained Christian, and those who came there mostly adapted it, at least after being there awhile. In many ways this was typical of how conversion to Christianity among the Norse and Vikings progressed: It was first adapted by leaders and royal rulers for practical strategic purposes, then later adapted by common people as they became more assimilated with their fellow Europeans. By the end of the eleventh century, nearly all Norse people in all parts of the world had become Christians.

It was not surprising that the Normans would set up a monarchy to rule their homeland; kingdoms headed by families that transferred power from one generation to the next were common in Scandinavia by that time. However, Rollo and his successors took passionately to the pomp and ceremony of European royal custom, and adeptly constructed a feudal system of lords and vassals in a chain of command under the ruling duke to administer their territories, just like the hierarchies found in other, long-established Frankish kingdoms. They imitated the dress, style, and mannerisms of their new neighbors, and some say they even elevated them to higher levels of sophistication. Cultural conversion was not limited to just royalty, though. A huge influx of Scandinavians and people of Norse heritage immigrated to Normandy during the rest of the tenth century. Sometimes these new arrivals would maintain their native ways, and in sections of Normandy distinctive Norse traits and characteristics were kept alive. Nevertheless, Normandy continued to blend into western Europe, demonstrating vividly the Norse tendency toward social and cultural assimilation. In fact, the Normans' adaptation skills were so great that they came to excel among their mainland European peers, spreading their influences among the dominant European populace. For example, the modern nation-state of France was effectively created at the end of the Frankish civil war out of the western portion of the old empire. Yet many historians believe modern French culture and national identity have been more influenced by Normandy than by any other region or subpopulation group, even though Normandy did not emerge as a separate entity until a century later.

The Normans also became militarily powerful and territorially expansionist. Over the following centuries, they built a confederation of landholdings that resembled a modern-day commonwealth. These lands stretched from the Middle East, where the Normans were major players in the Crusades of the twelfth century, to Britain, where they gained stature as the last foreign power ever to conquer England. They also established large territorial holdings in Italy, and the collective Norman influence there as well as in England and France played a major role as the Renaissance art and cultural movement emerged in the following centuries. The predominant western European culture that was to emerge during the Renaissance and Reformation periods and which is still prevalent in modern times owes a lot to Norman contributions.

REMNANTS OF A VIKING HERITAGE

In *The Viking Saga*, Peter Brent contends that the Normans' inclination toward conquest and expansion reflects an ongoing dichotomy between their adapted Frankish customs and society and their Viking heritage:

> Within the body politic of France Normandy had settled, rooted so deeply that later generations never thought

about its people's Scandinavian origins. . . . But the energy which drove them deep into the Mediterranean basin on their campaigns of conquest was doubtless the same as that which had carried the Vikings across the oceans and along the river valleys of the Western world. For that reason the alterations to the maps and cultures of Europe for which the Normans were responsible is a part of that complex legacy which the Northmen left behind them.[42]

Besides a continued emphasis on personal enrichment and ongoing territorial expansion, other Viking characteristics persisted in Norman culture. The same inclination shown by the Vikings in England and Ireland to use their landholdings to set

THE NORMANDY-ENGLAND CONNECTION

Relations between the newly formed province of Normandy and England were tense during the late ninth century, as many of the Vikings who had resumed heavy raiding in England took refuge in Normandy. A formal agreement between the two principals put an end to that practice, and England and Normandy became more closely connected in the following years.

English king Ethelred sought and received refuge in Normandy during the invasion and conquest of England by Svein Forkbeard. During his exile he married Emma, a daughter of Norman duke Richard I, William the Conqueror's grandfather. After Ethelred's return to England, his failure to hold the throne to which he had been reinstalled, and his subsequent death, Canute, as king, married the widowed Emma. Thereby Emma, of Norman origin, maintained the title of queen of England.

King Edward, who would assume the throne of England in 1042 after the deaths of Canute's heirs, was the son of Ethelred and Emma. This made Edward and Duke William cousins. During his reign in England, Edward showed great favoritism in his dealings with William and the Normans, and the two became close allies. The relationship that had developed between the ruling families of England and Normandy was the basis upon which Duke William laid claim to the English throne. Norman historical sources claim that William and Edward had agreed that whichever of them predeceased the other, the survivor would rule both England and Normandy.

up vibrant trade areas that drew people from great distances was well evident in Normandy. The stress placed by Vikings on skill and talent in art and craftwork was likely a major factor in the rapid and far-reaching development of Norman culture and literacy. The diplomatic and political skill displayed by Vikings in forging alliances with other tribes, kingdoms, or state-level governments in Britain and elsewhere in the world was also a cultural strength of the Normans. These distinctive Viking tendencies were generally more subtle than the overt adaptation of the native language, religion, customs, and the officially proclaimed alliance with mainland Europe. Nevertheless, Normandy's Viking origins seem to have had an underlying energizing effect on its population and institutions and played a major role in propelling Normandy to a position of high prominence in the world.

History professor R. Allen Brown, author of *The Normans,* says of them that they "were in the end to adapt themselves out of existence."[43] Brown refers to the long-term incorporation of Norman culture throughout France, England, and much of western Europe that occurred simultaneously with Normandy's absorption into France and the Norman people's absorption into native populations in their territories. This inclination toward cultural and social assimilation is perhaps the single most prominent Viking cultural trait maintained by the Normans. This tendency was clearly evident in the Viking territories in England and in Ireland during the later part of the Viking era. It can also be found among the Vikings who raided, conquered, and settled in the eastern European territories that were to become Russia and Ukraine. The trend among rulers within Scandinavia to adapt and imitate the manners, customs, and governing systems found in mainland Europe as the Viking era progressed has been extensively noted by historians. But the Normans' quick and far-reaching cultural conversion is more than just typical of Norse peoples; it actually distinguishes them as being ahead of their Scandinavian kinsmen in terms of affiliating with the larger European and international community.

THE RISE OF DUKE WILLIAM

Over a century after Rollo and the first Viking settlers founded Normandy, it came under the rule of perhaps the most famous Norman ever: Duke William, the famous William the Conqueror, a direct descendant of Rollo. Although thoroughly Frankish in his upbringing, appearance, and manner, William possessed those traits and characteristics historically associated with the Norse and Vikings that his predecessors had, such as territorial and wealth ambition and shrewd political and diplomatic ability.

He was an illegitimate heir to the previous duke and assumed the title at the very early age of eight. William faced opposition among the feudal overlords who ruled under the duke in Normandy. His moniker "the Conqueror" was first earned when he defeated the barons who sought

William the Conqueror expanded Norman territories by adding the provinces of Maine and Brittany to his domains.

In 1051, William had received the word of then English king Edward, who was childless, that he, William, would be named heir to the throne. William and Edward were related through a royal marriage that had taken place generations earlier, and William apparently made enough of an impression upon Edward that he named him as his successor. William also had been promised by Edward's brother-in-law, Harold Godwinsson, that he would not challenge his claim to the throne. That promise was obtained in 1064 at the meeting that took place between the two that proved to be so controversial. The circumstances under which Godwinsson made that promise could easily be called coercive—William reportedly was hospitable to Godwinsson but prevented his departure until he had made the promise. Indeed, Harold did not honor his word when presented with the opportunity to become king himself. This drew a response from William the Conqueror, who felt he was entitled to the English kingdom.

Besides Harold Godwinsson and William the Conqueror, a third major historical figure played a role in the events signifying the conclusion of the Viking era. That person was a Norwegian king named Harald Hardrada. Hardrada gained legendary status among the Vikings, largely through his ventures in eastern Europe and Constantinople, where Viking activities would prove to be as historically important as those in the British islands and western continental Europe.

to challenge his supremacy in Normandy and established firm control over the province, which he did over the course of the next two decades. Following this, William led the Normans to victory and conquest over the neighboring province of Maine to the south. Brittany also declared loyalty to William, mostly as a concession to avoid facing the same kind of conquest. With these triumphs William resumed large-scale territorial expansion of Normandy. He had his eye on a much larger place, though—Great Britain, across the English Channel.

Chapter

6 The Rise of Russia: Vikings in Eastern Europe and Byzantium

Vikings also traveled east during the Viking era. Just as they did in western Europe and Britain, Vikings raided, conquered areas, settled the land, engaged in trade and commerce, and assimilated with the local population in sections of eastern Europe that are now Russia and Ukraine. However, they did not follow the same pattern with these activities that they did in the west. Thomas S. Noonan, a history professor at the University of Minnesota, details some differences between eastern and western Europe at the start of the Viking era:

> Shallow-draught Viking boats could easily attack and plunder the rich towns and monasteries lying along the sea-coasts or river-banks of England and France, and make a successful get-away before local defenses could be organized. But there were no lootable towns or monasteries along the coasts of Russia, while the routes inland involved crossing dangerous rapids and portaging substantial distances through virgin forests to go from one river system to another. . . .

The geography of European Russia rewarded trading far more than raiding.

The Vikings in the west often did no more than take the treasure already accumulated in towns and monasteries. In European Russia, by contrast, the Scandinavians had to organize local systems to collect the natural wealth, and then establish trade centers and trading routes to market these goods.[44]

There is strong evidence that Norse people were pursuing just such a course of action, traveling great distances to the east and southeast, and settling and trading in some of those areas, for many years before any Viking raids occurred or Viking kingdoms were established in the ninth century. Yet raids and the creation of realms of power would also become a part of the Viking experience in eastern Europe, and that experience would also prove to be of great importance and lasting significance.

Russia, Ukraine, and other countries in easternmost Europe are primarily Slavic in culture and custom, but they have been strongly influenced by the Norse who came there over a millennium ago. In fact, the early formation of Russia can be traced to the Viking presence that was established there during

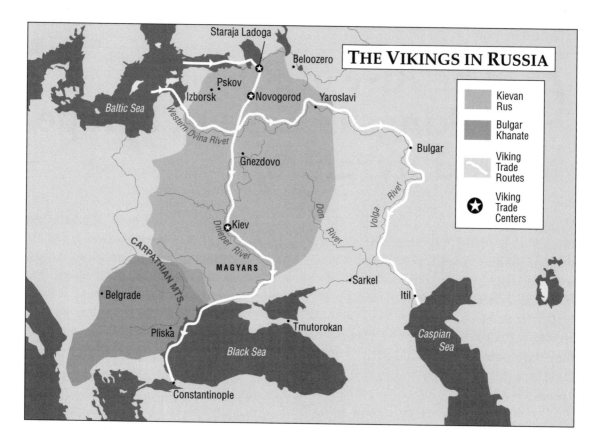

THE VIKINGS IN RUSSIA

Staraja Ladoga
Beloozero
Pskov
Izborsk
Novogorod
Yaroslavi
Baltic Sea
Western Dvina River
Bulgar
Gnezdovo
CARPATHIAN MTS.
Kiev
Dnieper River
MAGYARS
Don River
Volga River
Belgrade
Sarkel
Itil
Pliska
Tmutorokan
Black Sea
Caspian Sea
Constantinople

Kievan Rus

Bulgar Khanate

Viking Trade Routes

Viking Trade Centers

that time. The eastern European territories that the Vikings came to in the ninth century had a different history than Britain or western Europe. These areas had never been under the control of the Romans, nor had Christianity ever become the dominant or even a major religion. Prior to the Viking incursions into eastern Europe, tribal peoples known as Finns, Balts, and Slavs inhabited the area. To the east were Asian peoples known as Khazars, and to the south fierce nomadic tribes called Patzinaks. Occupying areas to the northeast and the west were the Bulgars. The territories in which these groups lived were important to the Vikings because they

provided access to major trading centers such as Baghdad, the center of wealth and trade in the Arab world; Constantinople, considered at that time to be the world's most wondrous city; and Bulgar, a city on the Volga River where goods from as far away as China could be obtained. Given the Viking craving for material riches, it was natural that they would set their sights on gaining access to these places.

Over the course of many years, the Vikings who traveled east came to dominate all the ethnic groups in the area and establish secure access to the trading centers and the routes that led between them and western Europe. However, unlike their counterparts in the west, they would exert force and gain dominance *after* already having settled in the area and cultivating social and commercial relationships with local populations.

RICHES TO THE EAST

Vikings in Russia were mostly Swedish. They had access to the interior of eastern Europe through a trade route that included the cities of Birka, on the east coast of Sweden, and Staraja Ladoga, at the mouth of the Volkhov River in what is now northwest Russia. Norse traders were regularly passing through these towns by the start of the Viking era, and the northern areas to the east of Scandinavia were often visited by the Vikings in search of Arctic animal furs, skins, and oils. The wealth to be gained in the eastern territories was readily attainable through trade, but as competition for power, wealth, and status among rival factions within Scandinavia became more intense, the lure of plundered loot led Vikings in eastern Europe to take these treasures by force. There were not the same kind of raiding targets to be found in these areas as in western Europe and Britain—excessive treasures concentrated within the bounds of monasteries and other Christian religious sites. This probably explains why Viking raiding in eastern Europe was never as intense as it was in the west. Still, the Balts and possibly Slavs had been subject to Norse raids at least sporadically for many years. In fact, the Balts were among the earliest victims of raids by Danish Vikings.

The increasing amount of riches moving through the eastern areas on the way to and from the trade centers provided greater incentive for raiding activity, and a major Viking raid on the town of Novgorod was recorded in the year 852. The Vikings seem to have effectively taken control of the town, but were persuaded to leave with a danegeld payment.

In 859 a Swedish noble named Rurik landed on the Baltic coast with a large fighting force. He had quite likely been prompted to come to the Baltics by stories of the successful Viking raids of Novgorod

Viking prince Rurik, founder and leader of the Russian Empire, is shown landing on the Baltic coast.

and other towns in the east. Rurik's forces are referred to in *The Russian Primary Chronicle* and other historical documents as the Rus, and it is widely believed that it is from this word that the nation name Russia was derived. The *Chronicle* claims the Rus were invited by several local factions to settle in the area and rule over them after a previous group of Viking infiltrators had been turned away. The entry for 862 states:

> The tributaries of the [Rus] drove them back beyond the sea and, refusing them further tribute, set out to govern themselves. There was no law among them, but tribe rose against tribe . . . and they began to war one against another. They said to themselves "Let us seek a prince who may rule over us and judge us according to the Law." They accordingly went overseas . . . then said to the people of Rus, "Our land is great and rich, but there is no order in it. Come to rule and reign over us!"[45]

Many historians doubt that the local tribal peoples made such a pointed request. Most likely this account was modified by the Rus who came to rule in Novgorod and other nearby cities to more favorably portray them. Then again, these tribes, all relatively primitive and militarily weak, may have seen the Rus as their best chance to reestablish the access to the major trading cities that was being disrupted by the Khazars and Patzinaks. Regardless of whether local Slavic tribes requested Rurik and the Rus to take charge or whether the Vikings acted on their own initiative, a strong Norse presence became rooted around the Volkhov River. Viking control of much of the Volga River valley to the east was also established under Novgorod's command.

The village of Kiev became a major Norse trading center in the 850s.

The Vikings had also been engaging in a combination of trading and raiding to the south, along the Dnieper River. They became more aggressive in the 850s when they greatly increased their raiding and captured the village of Kiev, turning it into a major Norse center. From Kiev the Vikings launched raids and exacted tribute from local tribes over a growing area that soon reached the Black Sea. To indicate their supremacy over others in the area, the Kiev rulers declared their sovereign to be the "Grand Prince" of Kiev. Control over the area was maintained by warriors who exhibited greater skill, ferocity, and success in battle than the tribal factions in the region. Unlike the Slavic tribes who had historically inhabited the area, these powerful Vikings were able to defend against and repel the Patzinaks, warlike nomads who lived in rugged terrain along the river. The Vikings' nautical skills helped them master the difficult rapids that ran in the Dnieper between Kiev and the Black Sea, the gateway to the Byzantine Empire. The Kiev Vikings effectively controlled the area and reaped the rewards of the rich flow of trade that ran through it.

QUELLING LOCAL TRIBES

The transition in the nature of the Viking presence from opportunistic raiding parties to regulated, organized armies that occurred in western Europe and Britain also took place in Kiev. Here it occurred rather quickly, as the earliest recorded raids in the area occurred within about a decade of the establishment of the principality centered in Kiev. Likewise, the town of Novgorod went from seeing opportunistic raiders in the early 850s to the highly sophisticated military units of Rurik in only about ten years. From power bases in Novgorod and Kiev, the might and efficiency of the Vikings came to dominate an area ranging far to the south and east.

Some local factions did resist Viking domination. A Slav tribe known as the Derevlians were not thoroughly subjugated by the Vikings until a vengeful widow named Olga brought about their downfall. Olga's husband, Igor, was a Norse ruler slain by the Derevlians. Seeking revenge, Olga headed a vicious campaign against the Derevlians in the mid-900s. Other Slavic tribes also resisted Rus dominance. *The Russian Primary Chronicle* refers to actions taken by the Rus against the Slavic Polyanians, Severians, Radimichians, the Ulichians, and the Tivercians as well as the Derevlians. The Rus also engaged in battle with the Turkish Khazar tribes, who had dominated much of the area prior to the Vikings' arrival. One in particular, the Khazar Qante, was not brought under Rus rule until well into the tenth century.

Beyond direct military action, the Vikings dominated local populations through superior force, collection of tribute, and indentured servitude in both the northern and southern regions of eastern Europe. The Viking reputation for ferociousness and slaughter may have preceded them among the Balts and Slavs, who had a history of interaction with

Viking Boats Travel by Land

As the Viking Rus came to dominate the Slavs and other local tribal peoples in eastern Europe, they had them perform many kinds of labor. One particularly fascinating task the Vikings needed performed was the portage of their boats across land from one river to another.

In the Russian territories, the Volkhov, Volga, and Dnieper Rivers, the main routes of transportation the Vikings needed to reach their destinations, did not connect with each other. So the Vikings needed to transport their vessels across land from one river to the next. Like the rivers themselves, the routes along which they conducted ship portage became major areas of settlement and development.

Once out of the water, the Vikings' ships may have been simply carried by hand, suspended upon wooden poles, or, in a particularly ingenious method of portage, rolled over the ground on top of wooden logs. Besides enabling them to get from one river to another, the ability to carry their ships out of the water was vitally important to the Vikings in their travels to and campaigns against Constantinople. The rocky rapids in parts of the Dnieper River required the Vikings to remove their ships and carry them around the impassable areas. When the Byzantines effectively blocked the Vikings' ships from entering the city's harbor during one of their attacks, the Vikings' were able to go around the blockade by bringing their ships onto land. The portage of their ships across land in the eastern territories is an excellent example of Viking adaptability and resourcefulness.

them, and this may have enabled the Vikings to gain dominance largely through sheer intimidation. Thomas S. Noonan has described the Vikings in Russia as being "Mafioso types seeking wealth and political dominance."[46] The overall combination of military, economic, intimidation, and diplomatic efforts undertaken by the Vikings in Russia clearly made them the dominant force there beginning in the mid–ninth century.

Constantinople and The Rise of Oleg

Some of the most dramatic and historically important Viking attacks were staged from eastern Europe. The focus of these attacks was Constantinople, the wealthiest and strongest city in the world at the time. Four of these attacks would take place between 860 and 944.

Heavily fortified and defended on land, Constantinople could be closely approached only by sea. Of course, as renowned sailors the Vikings were well equipped for and highly adept at this kind of operation. The first attack against the city was launched by a fleet of about two hundred ships. Constantinople was able to repel the Vikings, despite the fact that the Byzantine fleet was mostly out at sea. The leaders of the attack, lieutenants of Rurik named Askold and Dir, returned to Kiev to plan their next assault. As time wore on, they came to rule over Kiev, continuing to expand and strengthen the Viking holdings. However, they were not to get another opportunity to attack Constantinople.

The factional rivalry among the Norse that was common in Scandinavia and appeared in England between Norwegian and Danish Vikings also surfaced in eastern Europe. Askold and Dir were the victims of an ambush staged by the Novgorod ruler Oleg around 880. Oleg ruled Novgorod in the stead of Rurik's infant son after the original Rus conqueror's death. But Oleg proved to be very ambitious. During a campaign along the Dnieper River in which he captured two cities, Oleg proceeded to Kiev, where he slew Askold and Dir. *The Russian Primary Chronicle* describes this action:

> He [Oleg] then came to the hills of Kiev, and saw how Askold and Dir reigned there. He hid his warriors in the boats, left some others behind, and went forward himself bearing the child Igor. He thus came to the foot of

Oleg, ruler of Novgorod, defiantly nailing his shield to the gate outside of Constantinople.

the Hungarian hill, and after conceal-ing his troops, he sent messengers to Askold and Dir, representing himself as a stranger on his way to Greece on an errand for Oleg and for Igor, the prince's son, and requesting that they should come forth to greet them as members of their race. Askold and Dir straightaway came forth. Then all the soldiery jumped out of the boats, and Oleg said to Askold and Dir, "You are not princes nor even of princely stock, but I am of princely birth."[47]

After this, the *Chronicle* says that Oleg identified Igor as the son of Rurik, then had his men slay Askold and Dir. "Oleg set himself up as prince in Kiev," the pas-sage continues, "and declared that it should be the mother of Russian cities."[48] Oleg moved his base of operations there, and Kiev subsequently became the central city of the emerging Rus principality.

The Byzantines Bow to Viking Might

Oleg strengthened the Vikings' position in the east by fortifying defenses against the Khazars and the Patzinaks, and he estab-lished a ruling system consisting of a con-federacy of towns and provinces under the control of Norse princes. Oleg's quest for greater power, wealth, and status led him to again focus Viking attention on the mighty city of Constantinople, and the second Viking attack against that city took place in 907.

This time the assault was massive: eighty thousand warriors in cavalry units and two thousand ships. The Vikings plundered the relatively undefended out-lying areas of the city. They then moved their boats onto land to transport them around a huge chain the defenders had set up to prevent ships from entering the city's harbor. *The Russian Primary Chroni-cle* describes how "Oleg commanded his warriors to make wheels which they at-tached to the ships, and when the wind was favorable, they spread the sails and bore down upon the city from the open country."[49] This was enough to prompt the Byzantines to offer the Viking terms for peace. The Vikings would be granted ac-cess to the city with full trading rights if they called off their attack. Limitations were placed upon them, but the advan-tage of access to the trade and commerce of Constantinople was enough for the Vikings to accept the offer.

The agreement brought new strength to the Rus Viking confederacy, as the riches of Constantinople became available to them along with the trade routes leading to northern and western Europe. The Rus territories became as powerful and pros-perous as any settled and developed by the Vikings. Assimilation with the native tribes, especially the Slavs, had progressed substantially by the mid–tenth century, and the customs and culture of the people living in these areas were definitely tend-ing toward Slavic. Even the Rus rulers were becoming less distinctively Norse. However, they did remain ambitious, and after more than twenty years, they tried again to attack Constantinople.

In 941 Oleg's successor, Igor (who was to later be slain by the Derevlians), launched another offensive against the great city. This one was turned back by fire thrown by Byzantine vessels onto the open and unprotected boats of the Rus, who retreated from the city but ravaged the surrounding countryside. Like the areas of western Europe where Vikings looted, Byzantium had vast amounts of wealth and valuables within its territory, especially at sacred religious sites. The military forces of this empire were far superior to those of the kingdoms in western Europe, but they were not positioned throughout the countryside in such a way that they could defend against the Vikings, who sacked and burned churches and monasteries, plundered villages, took huge amounts of loot, and slaughtered hordes of people. Only in time did the Byzantines gather enough forces to stop the Rus wave of destruction. Yet it was not long until Igor rebuilt his forces and was launching an even stronger attack on the city in 944. This time fate took a hand as emissaries from Constantinople intercepted the Viking army. The Byzantine Empire urged Igor's forces not to attack but instead "accept the tribute which Oleg had received, and to the amount of which something should even be added."[50] Taken with the wealth, the Rus renewed their treaty, and the Vikings in Russia continued to benefit greatly from access to Constantinople.

Contact and trade between the Rus and the Byzantines were increased after this agreement, but there was one more major conflict between them. This occurred in the 960s, after Igor's son Svyatoslav had taken over as Rus ruler. The fighting centered on the territory of Bulgaria, where the Bulgars had been a common enemy of the Rus and Byzantines. At first Constantinople supported Svyatoslav when he

Byzantine weapons such as this fire thrower helped to defeat the Viking attack on Constantinople.

conquered the area with a large Rus army. However, when Svyatoslav then set up a new capital in the conquered territory and indicated he planned to concentrate large forces there, the Byzantines turned against the Rus and aligned themselves with the Bulgars. But the Rus marched on through Bulgaria and soundly defeated all the forces opposed to them, in spite of the presence of the powerful Byzantine army.

In the wake of this victory, Svyatoslav prepared to once again attack the empire to the south. He did offer to settle for peace in exchange for enormous ransoms for the newly taken territories and prisoners. There was a new emperor in Constantinople at this time named John Tzimisces, and he responded by dispatching the full might of the empire into Bulgaria against the Rus. A fleet of three hundred ships was dispatched to the mouth of the Danube River, and Svyatoslav's forces were driven out of their strategic position within Bulgaria. Finally the Rus surrendered and withdrew from Bulgaria. Yet all the while, the two sides kept their trade and access treaties intact, indicating that, whatever differences they may have had, they both recognized there were advantages in maintaining cooperation as well.

VLADIMIR AND THE CHRISTIAN CONVERSION

Shortly thereafter Svyatoslav was slain by the Patzinaks. His death set off years of civil conflict between his heirs, who divided up the Russian territory among themselves but fought for control over the whole domain. One of Svyatoslav's sons, Vladimir, held the title of prince of Novgorod. He left eastern Europe when the fighting broke out, after hearing that another of Svyatoslav's heirs, Oleg, had been killed by Yaropolk, who had assumed the prince's throne in Kiev. The death of Oleg and the fleeing of Vladimir left Yaropolk in sole control of the Rus territory. But Vladimir returned a few years later with a large army of Swedish Vikings, who were still accustomed to the fierce raiding and battling traditions of the native Norse. *The Russian Primary Chronicle* entry for the years 978–980 opens with this passage: "Vladimir returned to Novgorod with [Swedish] allies, and instructed the lieutenants of Yaropolk to return to the latter and inform him that Vladimir was advancing against him, prepared to fight."[51]

Through a combination of military might, cunning, and secret negotiations with members of Yaropolk's forces, Vladimir took power over the entire Russian principality in 980. He was as fierce and ruthless as his Rus predecessors had tended to be; the *Chronicle* describes Vladimir killing his rival to gain power, then attacking and subjugating many local tribes. Then again, he did stabilize the eastern European territories under his control as Kiev's prince. Under his rule, Rus relations with Byzantium were considerably more peaceful, especially after he adapted the Orthodox Christian religion of Byzantium as the official religion of Russia in 988. This gave the new emerging state considerably more stature

Vladimir's Religious "Auditions"

Prince Vladimir was not what one would consider a religious person when he took power in Kiev. He drank to excess and was known to have numerous wives and girlfriends in different places. Nevertheless, Vladimir realized that religion could help unite and strengthen a society, especially a new, emerging one like Russia, which was so ethnically diverse and divided by internal conflict.

When Vladimir was considering what religion to adopt for the Rus, representatives from major religions addressed him, trying to persuade him to join their religion. Muslim Bulgars were told their religion was unacceptable because of their abstinence from pork and, especially, alcohol. According to *The Russian Primary Chronicle,* Vladimir claimed drinking was "the joy of the Russes," and said of his people, "We cannot exist without that pleasure."

Roman Catholic representatives from central Europe and Jewish leaders from among the Khazars were also rejected: Vladimir disliked the Catholic practice of fasting and considered Judaism unworthy because the Jews had been driven out of their homeland in Jerusalem. "If God loved you and your faith, you would not be thus dispersed in foreign lands," he said.

Historians consider that Vladimir's ultimate decision to accept the Orthodox Christianity promoted by Byzantine representatives was more driven by practical national considerations than by any deep religious conviction. Viking Russia was much more economically dependent upon Constantinople than any of its other regional neighbors, and the advantages of accepting Orthodoxy were great. This conversion was critical in consolidating Russia as a nation-state and in the development of Russian culture.

among other large states and kingdoms that adhered to Christianity. It also helped unify the people of the Russian state. As a result of the Norse's conquests, subjugations, and absorption of local tribes and peoples, the Rus populace consisted of people with a wide range of ethnicities, traditions, and religious backgrounds, but as Thomas S. Noonan explains, "By accepting Orthodoxy from Byzantium, [the Rus] created a single faith for peoples who had nothing in common. Slavs, Finns, Balts, Vikings all now had one common faith."[52]

With the heightened contact between the two, Byzantine influence on the emerging Russian national culture was substantial. Just as the Normans adapted quickly to Christianity in western Europe and soon mastered a knowledge of the religion itself as well as the splendid art, craftsmanship, and literature associated with it, so, too, did the Russians in eastern Europe. Russia came to be a major cultural and political force in world history, just as Normandy did in the west. Prior to the Viking settlement and domination of the area, there was no centralized power, social or political structure, or military presence there that might have led to the development of such a major modern nation-state. The formation and development of the early stages of a Russian state is clearly one of the most important results of Viking military venturism. Russia has proven to be a dominant player in world affairs for several centuries, and has also been a major contributor to world art, culture, and society.

The Varangian Guard and King Harald Hardrada

At the same time Vladimir was converting Russia to Orthodox Christianity, he was also reaching a deal with Byzantine emperor Basil II regarding the use of Viking troops in the Byzantine army. Up to six thousand Vikings were dispatched to the service of the emperor, who formed a special force known as the Varangian Guard.

The emperor knew of the Vikings' great warrior prowess, but was also impressed by the loyalty traditionally shown by Vikings toward their chosen leaders. The performance of the Varangian Guard and the loyalty they showed to the emperor were renowned. Rus troops fought on behalf of Byzantium in campaigns in Europe and Asia for many years before the formation of the Guard. Although they primarily served as a personal security and personal service force for the emperor, the Varangian Guard also participated in the warfare undertaken by the Byzantines in the late tenth and eleventh centuries.

One Viking warrior to join the Varangian Guard was Harald Sigurtharson, who became better known as Harald Hardrada. He would later become king of Norway. Hardrada came to Kiev at age fifteen, after having fought on behalf of his half brother, the deposed Norwegian king Olaf II, in his Scandinavian homeland. At that time these kinds of internal conflicts were driving many noble and powerful Norse out of their homelands. Like Hardrada, they were seeking new opportunities for wealth and conquest abroad. After serving for a time among the palace troops at Kiev, Hardrada joined the Varangian Guard. "The Saga of Harald Sigurtharson" in the *Heimskringla* contains this passage:

> When Harald arrived in Byzantium and had had a meeting with the queen he took military service with her and right away . . . sailed with some galleys together with the fleet into the Greek Sea. Harald had command over a troop of his own men. . . . Harald had joined the expedition but a short time before the Varangians be-

came greatly attached to him, so they all fought together in battles. And at last Harald became the leader of all the Varangians.[53]

Under Hardrada's stewardship, the Guard enjoyed extensive success in campaigns on behalf of Byzantium. Hardrada is credited with capturing as many as eighty Arab cities during an excursion into Persia. He also won concessions from the Muslim rulers of Jerusalem permitting Christian access to the city, and conquered several strongly defended cities in Sicily. He gained great stature, wealth, and power, as well as gratitude from the Byzantine emperor.

Of course, during the time he was in the Varangian Guard, his conquests were not to benefit the Vikings, but they are a legendary part of Viking lore and illustrative of the Viking spirit of adventure and military prowess. Although a member of a ruling family, learned in the ways of the world and exposed to the highest levels of culture, Harald Hardrada is often cited as one of the last true prominent Vikings because of his many raiding and conquering ventures. His story's appearance in the *Heimskringla* has helped make him legendary.

Hardrada left the Varangian Guard when Basil II was replaced by Michael V. Hardrada and the new emperor did not get along, and Hardrada even went so far as to participate in a violent revolt against Michael. In the early 1040s Hardrada returned to Norway, celebrated and battle seasoned, with the intention of driving his nephew Magnus from the Norwegian throne. Like Vikings had done throughout their history, the two principals reached an agreement whereby each one gained: Magnus conceded half of Norway to Hardrada, who in turn bestowed half his worldly riches upon Magnus. When Magnus died in 1047, Hardrada became ruler over all of Norway.

Hardrada is the third of the three major historical leaders, along with English king Harold Godwinsson and Normandy's William the Conqueror, to participate in the important events that would symbolize the end of the Viking era. It was about twenty years after he took over Norway when this highly successful and ambitious ruler would turn his attention to the popular Viking target of England. In 1066, he launched an invasion of Great Britain that would be the first in a chain of monumental events in world history.

7 1066: The Vikings Bow Out

When Harald Hardrada invaded England in 1066, he did so with the intention of reclaiming the English throne that had been held by the line of Danish kings earlier in the eleventh century. Although of Norwegian origin, Hardrada had blood links to those kings, whose family had also come to rule over Norway. Under Danish kings, the presence and influence of the Danes in England had become great, but even before that the Norse presence and influence there had been growing for many years. In fact, the Norse had become so infused and prominent within English society that historical author R. Allen Brown has said, "In 1066, Anglo-Scandinavian rather than Anglo-Saxon may be thought the more appropriate description of the Old English Kingdom."[54]

This was reflected in the forces mustered to defend England against invasion. King Harold Godwinsson was partially Danish, and many of those loyal to him were likewise of mixed Anglo and Scandinavian origin. Actually, on both sides of the conflict that took place between Hardrada's Norwegian-led forces and Godwinsson's English loyalists, there was much more blending of heritages and na-

tional loyalties than there had been two hundred years earlier. In his attempt to reclaim England, Hardrada was aided by an English earl named Tostig, a brother of reigning English king Godwinsson. Tostig had been exiled from England and taken up residence in the Orkney Islands, and he had many loyal followers join him and Hardrada in their attempt to conquer England.

The forces assembled by Hardrada were awesome: between 250 and 300 ships, with possibly more than ten thousand men. These forces raided and plundered as they made their way along the British coast, eventually turning inland along the Humber River and toward the city of York. Initially the Norwegian-led alliance was successful when first engaged by an English force on the mainland led by two local earls. The armies met at the Battle of Fulford on September 20. "The Saga of Harald Sigurtharson" in *Heimskringla* describes the action:

> Ordering his banner Landwaster to be carried in front of him, he [Harald] made such a severe onslaught that everything gave way before him; and there was great loss among the men

of the earls, and they soon broke in flight, some fleeing upriver and others downriver, but most fled into the marsh, which became so filled up with their dead that the Norsemen could pursue them dry-shod.[55]

Following this, the English sent a message that they would surrender to Hardrada, and a meeting was set at which the English would recognize him as king and comply with other terms. Believing this to be the purpose of the meeting, Hardrada left a large part of his forces with the fleet on the river south of York when he went to Stamford Bridge, about seven miles east of the city, for his meeting with the English.

Hardrada was stunned to find he had walked into an ambush. An army led by King Godwinsson himself, and including a celebrated and powerful group of warriors known as Huscarls, greeted his unprepared forces. Harald's saga says that the Norse fought hard and that they came close to driving off the English, as Hardrada "fell into such a battle-fury that he rushed ahead of his men, fighting two-handed so that neither helmets nor mail corselets could withstand him, and all those who stood in his path gave way."[56] However, the Norwegian king was felled by an arrow to the throat. Following this, those among his troops who failed to retreat were also slain.

The Norse-led forces were then taken over by exiled earl Tostig, and reinforced by contingents from the ship fleet, who got word of the ambush and made a frantic effort to come to the aid of their fellows. According to the saga, by the time they reached the battle they were exhausted and were easily cut down by Godwinsson's army. *The Anglo-Saxon Chronicle* claims that the survivors "went inland to our king, and swore oaths that they would ever maintain peace and friendship with this land; and the king let them sail home with twenty-four ships."[57] The dramatic reduction in the number of ships in the fleet indicates the huge losses suffered by the Norwegian-led army.

WILLIAM IN THE WINGS

All the while, William the Conqueror was preparing his own invasion of England, having assembled a fleet and fighting forces along the western coast of the continent. William's forces were actually ready to set sail in August of 1066, but weather conditions prevented them. While the Norman troops were waiting for conditions to clear, the Norse-led forces had gotten to England first. Godwinsson's English forces had been expecting the attack from Normandy and been positioned in the south of England to defend against it. Since they had to divert much of their army a good distance to the north to defend against Hardrada, then return south, the English defenders were not well prepared to face the Normans.

With the English deployed to the north, the Norman forces faced no resistance when they crossed the English Channel. They landed in a town called Pevensey, then moved north to Hastings, where they set up a base. Word of the

Norman landing reached Godwinsson on October 1, and he immediately set out to meet the new invasion. Apparently Godwinsson's intention was to repeat the tactics he had used against Hardrada, moving rapidly from a great distance to take his adversaries by surprise. However, his forces did not adequately recover from their previous encounter, and Godwinsson moved so quickly back to the south that not all his remaining forces could keep pace with him. Also, Norman reconnaissance alerted William's forces about the approaching English army, thereby taking away the advantage of surprise the English were counting on.

Instead, the Normans began to move against the English on the morning of October 14, and Godwinsson's army was forced to take up defensive positions as they were nearing the Norman base. In retrospect, many historians believe the English forces made a mistake by rushing back south to face the Normans so soon. The two armies were roughly equal in number, about seven thousand men each, but the fatigue factor surely worked against the English. In spite of their disadvantages, Godwinsson's forces fought valiantly and, according to a written description by a Norman historian of the time, even gained the upper hand during the fight. This account of the battle by William of Poitiers claims that forces on one flank of the Norman army gave way and that the rest of the Norman forces also began to yield as a rumor spread that Duke William had been slain. According to Poitiers, William himself squashed the rumor by removing his helmet and baring his head, proclaiming loudly, "Look at me. I am alive, and by God's help, I shall win. What madness puts you to flight?"[58] Following this, the tide turned heavily in the Normans' favor. By day's end it was King Harold Godwinsson who had been

William the Conqueror's fleet crosses the English Channel on its way to invade England.

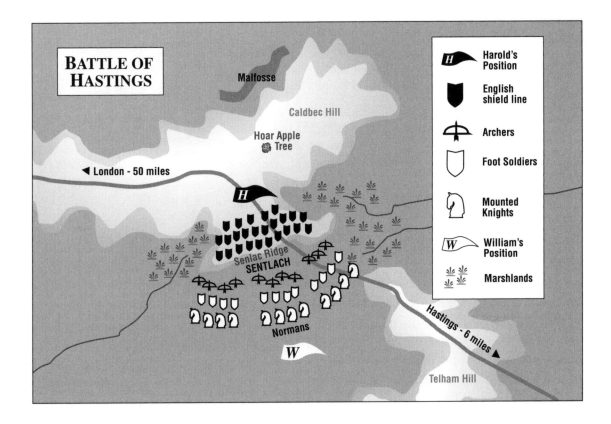

◀ London - 50 miles

BATTLE OF HASTINGS

Malfosse

Caldbec Hill

Hoar Apple Tree

Senlac Ridge
SENTLACH

Normans

Telham Hill

Hastings - 6 miles ▲

	Harold's Position
	English shield line
	Archers
	Foot Soldiers
	Mounted Knights
	William's Position
	Marshlands

slain, along with two of his brothers. The English forces had been decimated, and there were no leaders left among them with strength or prestige enough to rally or regroup them. Duke William had conquered England and was crowned king in London on Christmas Day of that year.

SYMBOLIC OR SIGNIFICANT TURNING POINT?

The year 1066 and the Battles of Stamford Bridge and Hastings are widely regarded as historically symbolizing the end of the Viking era. However, a great many changes that contributed significantly to the fading of the Viking era had occurred over the two previous centuries. The social and political structures in the Scandinavian homelands had evolved to where almost the entire area had come under the rule of just a few leaders. These leaders had created governing apparatuses that were more like the kingdoms of nation-states and empires than local or regional factional alliances. Many of the customs and ways of the mainland European lords and nobles had been adapted by the ruling classes in the Scandinavian countries that were consolidating and emerging along with other European nation-states.

The three armies that figured in the events of 1066 also displayed characteristics that further demonstrated changes and developments taking place during

William the Conqueror's victory at the Battle of Hastings signifies the end of the Viking era.

the Viking era that led to its conclusion. Similar to Svein Forkbeard's army in England during the first half of the eleventh century, the Viking forces were all large, composed of units organized in formal, hierarchical structures, and under the command of a powerful central leader who was also a major king or sovereign ruler. The early Viking raiding parties and even the large Viking armies that appeared in Europe during the mid–ninth century were smaller, informally organized, and acting either in their own collective interests or possibly on behalf of a small-scale chieftain or king. Furthermore, they were uniformly Norse in their makeup. Such was not the case by the eleventh century. Hardrada's forces, for example, included a sizable contingent of English opposed to the reigning king, demonstrating that alliances and loyalties in conflicts in Britain had crossed national, regional, and ethnic lines. Even King Godwinsson's English forces con-

sisted of many people, including nobles and royal-class warriors, who like the king himself were at least partially of Norse descent. This was indicative of both the degree of Viking assimilation within England and the levels of power and affluence that the Norse and their descendants had reached. Duke William's Norman forces were culturally mostly French. They were descended from the Norse and possibly still driven to ambition and expansion by their Viking roots and heritage, but they were a shining example of how thoroughly and effectively Norse immigrants and settlers could assimilate into and even become prominent within other societies and populations. The Norman army, like their whole population, represented a wide variety of national and regional origins and heritages.

Widespread assimilation of the Norse into other European populations resulted in a considerable blurring of the distinctive Norse and Viking identity that had

THE BAYEUX TAPESTRY

The Bayeux Tapestry is a masterpiece of art from the Middle Ages. It depicts the story of William the Conqueror's taking of the throne of England, beginning with the promise made to William by Harold Godwinsson not to challenge him for the throne through the defeat of the English forces at the Battle of Hastings. Although a brilliant and intricate work of ancient art, the tapestry uses a technique common to modern-day photo journals and comic books—captioning of illustrations—to tell its story.

Normandy had changed from its Norse origins and as a whole now more resembled a mainland European kingdom. However, the practice of making boldly colorful, intricate tapestries is one Norse tradition that survived in Normandy, and the Bayeux Tapestry exemplifies that. Another link to their Norse heritage is displayed in the ships shown in the Bayeux Tapestry that the Normans used to cross the English Channel. These vessels greatly resemble those associated with the Vikings. Notice the long, narrow, shallow boats with prows on both sides, made from long, thin overlapping planks, in these segments of the tapestry.

Of course, there's also that most notable of Viking trademarks—the ferocious dragonhead—that portrays just where the Normans' ship-making and seafaring talents originated.

In this segment from the Bayeux Tapestry the type of ship that the Normans sailed to England is shown.

become so prominent in the ninth and tenth centuries. By the second half of the eleventh century, there was nowhere among the places where the Vikings had raided, settled, and conquered that maintained prominent Norse cultural or societal features or characteristics. In western continental Europe, the only place where the Vikings had settled, established a strong presence that was both militarist and economic, drew travelers and trade activity from a large part of the world, and integrated with local populations was Normandy. By the late eleventh century, Normandy had become so prominent within mainland Europe that it was seen as defining and dominating the continent's culture to a large degree. Likewise in eastern Europe, substantial and distinctive signs of Norse culture did not remain by 1066. The ruling classes in the Russian and Ukraine territories were overwhelmingly Slavic- and Byzantine-influenced, even by the end of the tenth century, and the original Viking society was likewise largely absorbed by then.

In Ireland and Great Britain, a distinctive Viking presence persisted longer than on the mainland. Vikings and their descendants maintained some independent control over Dublin through the eleventh century. However, even before the last of the Viking rulers of Dublin died, the Vikings who had settled in Ireland had largely adapted and blended their customs and culture with those of the locals. Much the same can be said about those who migrated to the Viking areas of England, although the presence of massive Danish forces in England in the late tenth

and early eleventh centuries did result in a large, powerful, distinctively Norse presence remaining there longer than in other places. In both Great Britain and Ireland, some Viking-style raids continued into the twelfth century; however, these were minor, infrequent, and the work of a few remaining Norse renegades, most of whom lived in remote Atlantic islands, and refused to give up their old lifestyle and adapt to the new emerging societies in Scandinavia.

THE VIKING ACHIEVEMENT

The adoption of Christianity by the major Scandinavian leaders and the widespread acceptance and practice of this religion by Norse people was also a major contributing factor to the end of the Viking era. Christopher D. Morris of the University of Glasgow in Scotland states that with their Christian conversions the Norse people "became part of the mainstream European Christian community, thereby . . . losing their earlier Viking identity."[59] That the Vikings would give up their religion so readily when their objectives could be met in return is one of the most enlightening and interesting aspects of Viking behavior. In many of the places where the Vikings raided, plundered, and conquered, those who opposed them were Christians, and they considered the Vikings to be godless heathens. Of course, the Vikings' motivation in attacking sacred Christian sites was not religious hatred—when riches could be acquired more quickly and easily with

Journeys and Discoveries Across the Atlantic

Not everyone who ventured out of Scandinavia during the Viking era was a raider or warrior. Many Vikings voyaged to the lands east of Scandinavia to trade and settle, and even in the areas where Vikings attacked and conquered, many of the Norse people who came there did so to pursue trade, commerce, and the practice of their chosen craft.

Definitely one of the most important achievements of the Vikings was the westward exploration and settlement they undertook in the Atlantic Ocean. This began early in the ninth century, about the same time other Norse were starting the first raiding expeditions in Britain and Europe. The Shetland and Faeroe Islands in the North Atlantic were the first to be settled by Norwegian immigrants, followed by Iceland around 870. Today Iceland is an independent nation, and although very much a part of modern Western civilization, is probably the place where Viking culture and tradition have been most preserved. The ancient shipbuilding techniques of the Vikings are still practiced by many proud Icelanders, and although the country is overwhelmingly Christian, certain pagan rites and rituals that were a part of the Viking lifestyle have been ceremoniously preserved.

Beyond Iceland, Greenland was discovered and settled by Erik the Red in the late tenth century. *The Icelandic Sagas* tell of further explorations by Erik's son Leif to lands even farther west. The descriptions given in the sagas of the area visited by Eriksson are very similar to the east coast of Canada, but for many years there was no positive proof that Vikings had ever reached North America. In 1960 archaeological finds at L'Anse aux Meadows in Newfoundland proved that Vikings had in fact been the first Europeans to set foot in North America, nearly five hundred years before the arrival of Columbus.

The Vikings' stay in North America was a short one; the Native American tribes who already lived there had the Vikings outnumbered and outarmed. The settlements in Greenland also died out after a few hundred years, but the people who journeyed and settled there and in other new territories in the North Atlantic were just as much Vikings as those who raided and battled in Britain, Europe, and Byzantium.

a conversion to Christianity, the Vikings showed little resistance or reluctance to make that conversion.

The importance of the economic aspects of Viking culture must be emphasized in any historical review of the Vikings. The Vikings were most successful when they combined the force and military strength they may have needed to secure a presence in an area with the establishment and development of vibrant trade and commercial activity and extensive interaction with and cultural blending into the local populations. When the Vikings placed too much emphasis on the assertion of military force, they did not have a lasting impact. This can be seen in the first large-scale Viking occupation of Ireland and the Viking campaigns in Frankia during the ninth century. However, when the Vikings created successful trade and commerce and engaged actively in social and cultural integration, as they did during the second phase of Viking settlement in Ireland, in the north and east of England, in Normandy, and in Russia, the Vikings' presence had a lasting and important impact on those areas. In some cases the impact proved to be important in the history and development of the world as a whole—trade and commerce thrived in the North Atlantic as it never had before, and the newly formed societies of Normandy and Russia became powerful and influential states.

The stereotype of the Vikings as strictly brutish and savage raiders and warriors has recently been exposed as a misunderstanding of them as a people and a culture. To be sure, the Vikings were ferocious fighters, but the Viking culture was deep and rich, and the talents and characteristics they used to spread their influence and power went well beyond brute force and battle prowess. The Norse who set out from their homelands to the far reaches of the known world in the Viking era were steeped in a society with strong traditions in arts and crafts, farming, herding, foraging, shipbuilding and seafaring skills, and self-reliance and determination. As strong as their heritage was, they nevertheless proved adaptable to local conditions and customs, open and amiable to other peoples and societies, and diplomatically adept in their personal and political interactions with people and leaders from other societies. It was a combination of military venturism along with their other cultural strengths that enabled the Vikings to attain the levels of power and status they did during the ninth and tenth centuries and have a lasting impact on the world.

Notes

Introduction: Terror from a Pagan Race

1. Quoted in Colleen E. Batey and John Sheehan, "Viking Expansion and Cultural Blending in Britain and Ireland," in William Fitzhugh and Elizabeth Ward, eds., *Vikings: The North Atlantic Saga*. Washington, DC: Smithsonian Institution Press, 2000, p. 127.

Chapter 1: The Birth and Formation of Viking Culture

2. *The Anglo-Saxon Chronicle*. Trans. G.N. Garmonsway. London: J.M. Dent and Sons, 1953, pp. 54–57.

3. Helen Clarke, "Scandinavia Before the Vikings," in James Graham-Campbell, ed., *Cultural Atlas of the Viking World*. New York: Facts On File, 1994, p. 24.

4. Snorri Sturluson, "The Saga of the Ynglings," in *Heimskringla: History of the Kings of Norway*. Trans. Lee M. Hollander. Austin: University of Texas Press, 1964, p. 31.

5. Sturluson, "The Saga of the Ynglings," p. 23.

6. Quoted in Magnus Magnusson, *Hammer of the North: Myths and Legends of the Viking Age*. New York: G.P. Putnam's Sons, 1976, p. 13.

7. Magnus Magnusson, *Vikings!* New York: E.P. Dutton, 1980, p. 19.

8. Magnusson, *Vikings!*, p. 21.

Chapter 2: Early Invasions: Vikings Take Root in England and Ireland

9. *The Anglo-Saxon Chronicle*, pp. 62–63.

10. *Annals of St. Bertin*. Ed. and trans. Janet L. Nelson. Manchester, England: Manchester University Press, 1991, p. 61.

11. Peter Brent, *The Viking Saga*. New York: G.P. Putnam's Sons, 1975, pp. 19–20.

12. *Annals of Ulster: A Chronicle of Irish Affairs*. Ed. and trans. William M. Hennessy. Dublin, Ireland: Hodges, Figgis, 1887, p. 331.

13. *Annals of Ulster*, p. 347.

14. *Annals of St. Bertin*, p. 65.

15. *Annals of Ulster*, p. 417.

16. *The Anglo-Saxon Chronicle*, pp. 68–69.

17. *The Anglo-Saxon Chronicle*, pp. 68–69.

18. *The Anglo-Saxon Chronicle*, pp. 74–75.

19. Magnusson, *Vikings!*, p. 133.

20. *The Anglo-Saxon Chronicle*, p. 106.

Chapter 3: Viking Rule: A Dublin Dynasty and Danish Kings of England

21. *The Anglo-Saxon Chronicle*, p. 106.

22. *Annals of Ulster*, p. 491.

23. *Annals of Ulster*, p. 533.

24. Snorri Sturluson, "The Saga of Olaf Tryggvason," in *Heimskringla*, p. 169.

25. *The Anglo-Saxon Chronicle*, p. 129.

26. *The Anglo-Saxon Chronicle*, p. 141.

27. Magnusson, *Vikings!*, p. 270.

28. *The Anglo-Saxon Chronicle*, p. 152.

Chapter 4: Heights of Fury: Vikings in Frankia and the Western Continent

29. Quoted in Frank R. Donovan, *The Vikings*. New York: American Heritage Publishing, 1964, p. 12.

30. *Annals of St. Bertin*, p. 30.

31. Janet L. Nelson, "The Frankish Empire," in Peter Sawyer, ed., *The Oxford Illustrated History of the Vikings*, New York: Oxford University Press, 1997, p. 25.

32. *Annals of St. Bertin*, p. 51.

33. *Annals of St. Bertin*, p. 60.

34. Neil Price, "'Laid Waste, Plundered, and Burned': The Vikings in Frankia," in *Vikings: The North Atlantic Saga*, p. 121.

35. Quoted in Magnusson, *Vikings!* pp. 75–76.

36. *Annals of St. Bertin*, p. 131.

37. Brent, *The Viking Saga*, p. 55.

Chapter 5: Normandy: Viking Conquest at Its Best

38. Snorri Sturluson, "The Saga of Harald Fairhair," in *Heimskringla*, p. 79.

39. Sturluson, "The Saga of Harald Fairhair," p. 79.

40. Quoted in R. Allen Brown, *The Normans*. New York: St. Martin's Press, 1984, p. 166.

41. Quoted in R.H.C. Davis, *The Normans and Their Myth*. London: Thames and Hudson, 1976, p. 56.

42. Brent, *The Viking Saga*, p. 235.

43. Brown, *The Normans*, p. 9.

Chapter 6: The Rise of Russia: Vikings in Eastern Europe and Byzantium

44. Thomas S. Noonan, "Scandinavians in European Russia," in Sawyer, ed., *The Oxford Illustrated History of the Vikings*, p. 135.

45. *The Russian Primary Chronicle*. Ed. and trans. Samuel Hazzard Cross and Olgerd P. Sherbowitz-Wetzor. Cambridge, MA: The Mediaeval Academy of America, 1953, p. 59.

46. Quoted in *The Vikings* (videocassette), PBS Nova Series. Boston: WGBH, 2000.

47. *The Russian Primary Chronicle*, p. 61.

48. *The Russian Primary Chronicle*, p. 61.

49. *The Russian Primary Chronicle*, p. 64.

50. *The Russian Primary Chronicle*, p. 73.

51. *The Russian Primary Chronicle*, p. 91.

52. Quoted in *The Vikings* (videocassette).

53. Sturluson, "The Saga of Harald Sigurtharson," p. 79.

Chapter 7: 1066: The Vikings Bow Out

54. Brown, *The Normans*, p. 14.

55. Sturluson, "The Saga of Harald Sigurtharson," p. 649.

56. Sturluson, "The Saga of Harald Sigurtharson," p. 655.

57. *The Anglo-Saxon Chronicle*, p. 198.

58. Quoted in Brown, *The Normans*, p. 66.

59. Christopher D. Morris, "The Viking Age in Europe" in Fitzhugh and Ward, eds., *Vikings: The North Atlantic Saga*, p. 102.

For Further Reading

Yves Cohat, *The Vikings, Lord of the Seas.* New York: Abrams, 1992. Extensively informative regarding the Vikings' superb shipbuilding, seafaring, and navigational abilities.

George Constable, ed., *Scandinavia.* Amsterdam: Time-Life Books, 1985. Contains geographical as well as historical information about the five nations of Scandinavia and the region as a whole.

Mike Corbishley, *Vikings at a Glance.* New York: Peter Bedrick Books, 1998. Formatted to emphasize art and illustration, this book nevertheless contains substantial information about the Vikings and their culture.

Jim Gallagher, *The Viking Explorers.* Philadelphia: Chelsea House Publishers, 2001. Covers the westward exploration across the Atlantic by the Icelandic settlers Erik the Red and Leif Eriksson.

Shirley Glubok, *The Art of the Vikings.* New York: Macmillan, 1978. Looks at Norse artwork during the years 800–1100, roughly coinciding with the Viking era.

John and Louise James, *How We Know About the Vikings.* New York: Peter Bedrick Books, 1997. With a strong emphasis on archaeological evidence, this book examines ways and methods historians use to gain knowledge about the Viking era. Includes evidence uncovered by the most recent archaeological research.

Susan M. Margeson, *Viking.* New York: Alfred A. Knopf, 1994. Most of the text in this vividly graphic book is in photo and illustration captions, but it does present a thorough examination of Norse customs, culture, and lifestyle.

Philip Neil, *Odin's Family: Myths of the Vikings.* New York: Orchard Books, 1996. For younger readers, this book presents traditional Viking mythical tales featuring the Norse deities in a simple, modern style.

Robert Nicholson and Claire Watts, *The Vikings.* New York: Chelsea House Publishers, 1994. While not providing great detail, the Journey into Civilization series does include with each volume a recipe or craft activity, as well as an indigenous story or legend.

Robin Place, *The Vikings: Fact and Fiction.* Cambridge: Cambridge University Press, 1985. Uses a fictional story about everyday life in York among the Vikings to present information gathered from the extensive archaeological work done there. Includes extensive photos of artifacts, diagrams, and other graphics.

Nova, "The Vikings": www.pbs.org/wgbh/nova/vikings. PBS website for the program *Nova.* Includes a video tour of the trade village of Birka in Sweden, a section on the construction of Viking ships and archaeological discoveries of those ships, and an interactive map that includes information on many important Viking locations.

Works Consulted

Books

The Anglo-Saxon Chronicle. Trans. G.N. Garmonsway. London: J.M. Dent and Sons, 1953. Ancient text chronicling events in Britain, particularly England, and elsewhere during the Middle Ages.

Annals of St. Bertin. Trans. and ed. Janet L. Nelson. Manchester, England: Manchester University Press, 1991. Ancient text chronicling events in Frankia and elsewhere during the Middle Ages.

Annals of Ulster: A Chronicle of Irish Affairs. Ed. trans. William M. Hennessy. Dublin, Ireland: Hodges, Figgis, 1887. Ancient text chronicling events in Ireland and elsewhere during the Middle Ages.

Peter Brent, *The Viking Saga.* New York: G.P. Putnam's Sons, 1975. A dramatic, highly literary, far-reaching account of the Viking era.

R. Allen Brown, *The Normans.* New York: St. Martin's Press, 1984. Complete history of Normandy with an emphasis on the period leading up to and including the reign of William the Conqueror.

R.H.C. Davis, *The Normans and Their Myth.* London: Thames and Hudson, 1976. History of Normandy from the arrival of the first settler-warriors through the conquest of England, with a strong focus on the mythical aspects of Norman history and culture.

T.K. Derry, *A History of Scandinavia.* Minneapolis: University of Minnesota Press, 1979. Focuses more on recent developments in Scandinavia, but chronologically covers the initial formation of Norse society through the Christian conversion and the rise of the major national kingdoms. Puts the Viking age into an overall perspective.

Frank R. Donovan, *The Vikings.* New York: American Heritage Publishing, 1964. Somewhat dated and occasionally inaccurate, this book nevertheless provides a good basic overview of the important Viking ventures in different parts of the world. Includes many high-quality photographs of artifacts and exhibits.

William Fitzhugh and Elizabeth Ward, eds., *Vikings: The North Atlantic Saga.* Washington, DC: Smithsonian Institution Press, 2000. Heavily illustrated with photos of Viking artifacts, exhibits, illustrations, and maps, this book's release accompanied a Smithsonian exhibit in honor of the millennial anniversary of the Viking voyage to North America.

James Graham-Campbell, ed., *Cultural Atlas of the Viking World.* New York: Facts On File, 1994. An interdisciplinary volume that covers all aspects of the Vikings, with abundant photographs, drawings, and maps.

Michael Hart, *The 100: A Ranking of the Most Influential Persons in History.* New York: Galahad Books, 1982. A fascinating overview of world history in which the author ranks the most important people who have ever lived in order of how much influence they had on the course of history. The writing is simple and lucid. This book is an excellent starting point for anyone researching a major historical figure.

Ian Heath, *The Vikings*. London: Osprey Publishing, 1985. Briefly covers the Viking ventures in England, Ireland, and Russia, with additional information on various aspects of Viking culture and lifestyle.

Kathryn Hinds, *The Vikings*. Tarrytown, NY: Marshall Cavendish, 1998. A comprehensive examination of the Norse that focuses mostly on their lifestyle, society, culture, and beliefs.

Magnus Magnusson, *Hammer of the North: Myths and Legends of the Viking Age*. New York: G.P. Putnam's Sons, 1976. An examination of Norse mythical beliefs and their various gods. Also looks at the adoption of Christianity by the Norse and the relationship between their religious beliefs and their overall culture.

Magnus Magnusson, *Vikings!* New York: E.P. Dutton, 1980. A comprehensive examination of the Vikings, their origins, ventures and conquests, and their lasting impact and historical importance.

Hazel Mary Martell, *The Vikings*. New York: New Discovery Books, 1992. A clear, concise, comprehensive overview of the Viking era and the Norse culture and lifestyle from which it arose. Includes many high-quality photographs and maps.

Rosamond McKitterick, *The Frankish Kingdoms Under the Carolingians 751–987*. Burnt Mill, UK: Longman Group, 1983. Includes accounts of the Vikings' activities and importance in Frankia during the period covered, with a section focusing on Normandy and Brittany.

Else Roesdahl and David M. Wilson, eds., *From Viking to Crusader*. New York: Rizzoli International Publications, 1992. Traces the evolution and development of the Vikings primarily through their artwork, crafts, tools, and other archaeological artifacts.

The Russian Primary Chronicle. Ed. trans. Samuel Hazzard Cross and Olgerd P. Sherbowitz-Wetzor. Cambridge, MA: The Mediaeval Academy of America, 1953. Ancient text chronicling events in Russia from 852 to 1116.

A.J. Otway Ruthven, *A History of Medieval Ireland*. New York: Barnes and Noble, 1968. A general history of Ireland during the medieval period, including coverage of the Vikings' ventures and involvement there.

P.H. Sawyer, *Kings and Vikings: Scandinavia and Europe*. New York: Methuen, 1982. Fully examines Viking ventures and the development of Scandinavian spheres of influence during the Viking era.

Peter Sawyer, "The Vikings and Ireland," in David Dumville, Rosamond McKitterick, and Dorothy Whitelock, eds., *Ireland in Early Mediaeval Europe*. Cambridge: Cambridge University Press, 1982. Actually deals with the overall Viking presence in the Atlantic and how the Viking settlements in Ireland fit into it.

Peter Sawyer, ed., *The Oxford Illustrated History of the Vikings*. New York: Oxford University Press, 1997. A comprehensive examination of the Vikings, with colorful photos and illustrations.

Henry L. Snyder, "From the Beginnings to the End of the Middle Ages," in Harold Orel, ed., *Irish History and Culture*. Lawrence: University Press of Kansas. Discusses the Vikings in Ireland in context of that country's overall history during the medieval period.

Snorri Sturluson, *Heimskringla: History of the Kings of Norway*. Trans. Lee M. Hollander. Austin: University of Texas Press, 1964. The translated texts of the original historic Icelandic compositions.

Martin Windrow, *The Viking Warrior*. New York: Franklin Watts, 1984. Touches upon various aspects of Viking warfare and the way of life experienced by Viking raiders, warriors, and travelers.

Periodicals

Archaeology's Dig, "Gods of the Vikings," October/November 2000. Brief descriptions of some of the Norse deities.

Michael Klesius, "Mystery Ships from a Danish Bog," *National Geographic*, May 2000. Focuses on a pre–Viking era Norse ship recovered in Denmark.

David Schaffer, "The Adventurous Vikings," *Archaeology's Dig*, October/November. An overview of Viking history based on archaeological evidence.

Priit J. Vesilind, "In Search of Vikings," *National Geographic*, May 2000. An overview of the Viking period, with site reports from several important locations in Viking history.

Videocassette

The Vikings (videocassette), PBS Nova Series. Boston: WGBH, 2000. A wide-ranging look at Viking history and culture that includes interviews with numerous Viking scholars and experts.

Index

Svyatoslav, 87–88
Sweden, 14, 46, 51, 81–83
Swedes. *See* Sweden

Tacitus, 20
Tara, Battle of, 42
Thor, 15, 17, 74
Tiu, 17
Tostig, 92, 93
Tryggvason, Olaf, 46, 47
Turgeis, 29
Turkey, 83
 see also Byzantine
  Empire;
  Constantinople
Tzimisces, John, 88

Ukraine. *See* Russia

Valhalla, 15
Valkyries, 15
Varangian Guard, 90–91
Vikings
 archaeological findings
  and, 24, 99
 armies of, 33–36, 57–58,
  59, 65–67
 assimilation of, into
  conquered areas'
  cultures, 96–97
 bribes of, 47–48, 59–61
 brutality of, 11–12, 27,
  33

characteristics of
 civilization, 12
Christianity and, 70–71,
 74, 88–89, 98
days of the week names
 and, 17
definition of term, 20
economic impact of,
 98–99, 100
exploration and, 99
end of, 95–98
gods and goddesses of,
 17
government structure of,
 96
horses and, 33, 62
importance of, 13, 17, 90,
 100
payments to, 47–48,
 59–61
rivers and, 81, 82, 83
raids and settlement in
 England of, 32–36
religion of, 99
shipbuilding methods of,
 99
ships of, 22–24
tactics of, 60, 83
trading and, 34–35, 41,
 42–43, 67, 98
trickery of, 60
warlike qualities of,
 18–19

values and goals of,
 20–22
Viking Saga, The (Brent),
 29, 66–67, 75–76
Vladimir, 88–90
Volga River, 80, 82
Volkhov River, 81–82

Walcheren, 56–57
Wales, 31, 38
Waterford, 30, 36
Wessex, 32, 34, 36
Wickford, 30
William (duke of
 Normandy). *See* William
 the Conqueror
William Longsword. *See*
 Longsword, William
William of Poitiers, 94
William the Conqueror, 52
 conquest of England by,
  94–95
 coronation of, 95
 end of Viking era and, 91
 invasion of England of,
  93
 personal characteristics
  of, 77
 territorial expansion in
  Frankia and, 78

York, 33, 34–35, 38, 41,
 92–93

Picture Credits

Cover: Peter Newark's Historical Press

© Archivo Iconografico, S.A./CORBIS: 63

© Bettmann/CORBIS: 45, 66, 81

Gianni Dagli Orti/CORBIS: 71, 97

© Ted Spiegel/CORBIS: 30

© CORBIS: 26

Chris Jouan: 21, 25, 80

North Wind Picture Archives: 10, 12, 15(all), 28, 34, 47, 49, 62, 72, 78, 82, 85, 87, 94, 96

Scala/Art Resource: 19, 54

About the Author

David Schaffer has edited and designed books and magazines for young readers for the past seventeen years. A graduate of Skidmore College and the New York University Publishing Institute, he has written magazine and newspaper articles on history, entertainment, travel, politics, and social problems confronting young people. He first became interested in writing about the Vikings during the millennial celebration of the discovery of North America by Viking Explorer Leif Eriksson.

After spending most of his life in the New York City and Boston areas, he now lives in upstate New York with his wife and daughter.